PRAISE FOR
OFF MY KNEES

"Julie D. Summer's *Off My Knees* is a compelling memoir about overcoming abuse, addiction, and time in prison...(it) is about a confident personal reinvention."
— Carolina Ciucci, *Foreword Reviews*

"A gripping memoir detailing betrayal, trauma, prostitution, grief, drug addiction, imprisonment, the breaking force of love, detox and much more, all heightened by oscillating poverty...In OFF MY KNEES, FROM SKID ROW TO SUNSET BOULEVARD, Julie D. Summers discloses the story of her life, presenting the extent of human anguish, and rage, with phenomenal brutality. Both a rousing cautionary tale and a haunting confession, the memoir serves as a soothing word uttered to all those enduring the ache of existence."
— *IndieReader Reviews*

"This clear-eyed memoir faces addiction, abuse, and incarceration as it reveals a life that finds purpose in helping others."
— *Booklife Reviews*

"Off My Knees" is a front row seat at a powerful transformation that we all have the ability to create; a transformation that comes about not from magic, but from tapping into a deep well of divinity within us all.
— Joanna McAtee

"After hitting rock bottom following a life marred by sexual assault, addictions, prostitution, and imprisonment, Julie D. Summers survived the stormy years and later thrived in her pursuits. She documents her moving experiences in her memoir, *Off My Knees: From Skid Row to Sunset Boulevard*...readers seeking motivation to change their lives will find hope and strength in Summers's powerful story."
— *Blueink Review*

"*Off My Knees* is captivating and inspirational. Julie's descriptions and picturesque style of writing beautifully draw you into her world. I rode along the journey completely fascinated, wanting to know more. For me, this book is an illustration of the ultimate human experience called the hero's journey…where vulnerability is the backbone of strength and courage and is fundamental to reclaiming one's personal power."
— Lauri Westfall Ishihara

"A woman fights to overcome drug dependence as well as repair frayed relationships in this debut memoir. Summers, who's currently on the governing board of the nonprofit People Assisting the Homeless, describes an idyllic childhood in Pennsylvania. …Her life reached (a) turning point when she became pregnant as a teenager in 1965 and adults convinced her to give the baby up for adoption. A short time later, when she wanted to find her son, she took up sex work in order to be able to pay steep legal fees. Her life spiraled into habitual use of drugs, including prescription pills and meth. Things started looking up, though, when she began dating an encouraging, wealthy man, though he was married. She became an active community member in West Hollywood but continued to struggle with family relationships, particularly with her mother and her mentally ill son. Summers manages to pack a lot into this brief remembrance The author ends her book with a "self help guide" and a collection of personal musings to inspire readers to tackle their own problems.

"A refreshingly honest and intimate account of a troubled life."
— *Kirkus Reviews*

OFF MY KNEES

FROM SKID ROW TO SUNSET BOULEVARD

A True Story

Julie D. Summers

Off My Knees: From Skid Row to Sunset Boulevard

Copyright © 2022 Julie D. Summers

First Edition, September 2022

Published by The Book Store On Main Street 8
Los Angeles, CA

All rights reserved. No part of this book may be used or reproduced in any form by any electronic or mechanical means (including photocopying, recording, or information storage and retrieval) whatsoever without permission in writing from the author, except in the case of brief quotations embodied in critical articles and reviews.

Trademarks—All brand names and product names referred to in this book are registered trademarks and unregistered trade names of their owners. There is no implied endorsement of any of them.

Disclaimers—This novel is a work of creative non-fiction and is based on a true story. The events are portrayed to the best of the author's memory, some of which is already public record. While all the stories in this book are true, some names and identifying details have been changed to protect the privacy of the people involved. Neither the publisher nor the author shall be liable for any loss of profit or any other damages, including but not limited to special, incidental, consequential, or other damages.

Cover artist: Eric Labacz
www.labaczdesign.com/

Author cover photo by Jordan Ring Photography
www.jordanringphotography.com

ISBN 978-0-578-97107-0 Paperback Edition
ISBN 978-0-578-25242-1 Digitaal Edition
ISBN 978-0-578-25241-4 Hardcover Edition

Library of Congress Control Number: 2022915725

Printed in the United States of America

v18

This book is dedicated to people
who have experienced a tragedy beyond anything
they thought they could handle.

To those people who are in jail or prison,
to drug addicts who want to come clean,
to people who have experienced the death of a child,
and to those who are in economic distress.

And to anyone trying to make a better life.

CONTENTS

1. Childhood 1
2. Youth 21
3. The Baby and Prostitution 44
4. Los Angeles 66
5. Meth Addiction and The Hells Angels 79
6. Jail 90
7. Prison and Parole 105
8. Meeting Aris Anagnos, and E.J.'s Death 131
9. The Apartment Building, Living in West Hollywood 145
10. Meeting My Son 156
11. People Assisting the Homeless, John in Florida and Denver 167
12. The Final Mistress Years, John in Texas 177
13. John, My Son John 190
14. Detox and Rebirth 203
A Self-Help Guide 208
Thoughts 210
Acknowledgments 218

Chapter One

CHILDHOOD

The eclipse on June 7, 1947 heralded my entry into the world at 7:47am in Meadville Pennsylvania. My parents, Don and Evalyn June Essig, named me Diana Rae. Meadville was the quintessential American town, prosperous, safe, and wholesome, very close to the Zenith in Sinclair Lewis' book "Babbitt." Like many baby boomers, my childhood was idyllic, playing in the postwar security that turned small towns into dreamlands.

The 1950's ushered in the golden age of America, a land of plenty that smelled of opportunity with the promise of prosperity for all. Having a population of about 20,000 people, Meadville was the home of Talon Zippers, the first zipper factory in America, and this factory provided a good living for the townspeople.

I like to think my ancestors settled in Meadville because it reminded them of their homeland, the wooded green of Germany and Ireland. Being the fourth generation to raise families in Meadville gave my parents stability and a history of existence. A physically beautiful woman, my mother Evalyn June, or E.J. as she liked to be called, was 5'7" with the figure of a movie star. She used lipstick and Heaven Sent perfume, although every perfume smelled good on her. A man's woman who wore her sexuality well, she took the role of wife seriously and played the role of mother as if she had read it from a book. The house was always clean, the meals cooked, and the beds changed once a week with sheets freshly blown dry in the outside air. The only thing missing was her emotion. For this she had good reason, as she was born an only child during the Great Depression and her mother, Charlotte, put Mama into an orphanage when she was five.

Mama's father's name was Buck First. I met my grandfather once, when I was about six. Passing through town, he wanted to meet each of us children, but especially me. He kept saying "She looks exactly like Charlotte." He did not get a chance to say this very often as we met in the Florida porch of our house, not the living room, and my father never left my side. Grandfather Buck, a man tortured by drink, drifted away to Mexico after Charlotte died, and I never saw him again.

Mama told me terrible stories of the orphanage. Children who had misbehaved would be lined up and then swung in front of the open fire in the basement furnace and told they would be thrown into the fire and burned if they misbehaved again. Mama had been in the orphanage for a year when her mother died.

When Mama was seven, her Uncle Ken and his wife, Irene, took her from the orphanage to live with them. Uncle Ken became her foster father. He was an evil man who raped her repeatedly, starting when she was thirteen or fourteen.

When her father, Buck, came to town, he telephoned his brother Ken and asked to see Mama. Buck and Mama met on the bank of a nearby river. She told her father of the repeated rapes and asked him for help. "Go back," he told her. "There is no other place for you to live." Buck continued his travels around the country. No one knew where he was or what he was doing. My mother was abandoned again.

She cracked at a very young age—not completely cracked, but like Humpty Dumpty, she could not be put back together again. For the rest of her life, it seemed she was trying to live a storybook life, probably so she could bury her past by feeling perfect.

Six feet tall, lanky, and twelve years older than my mother, my father, Don, was raised as a gentleman. He cut a dapper figure, with style and sophistication. Soft-spoken and gentle, he never spanked me nor raised his voice to me. I always felt his gentle strength through his deep, pure love for me.

∴

My parents met in Meadville when Daddy was singing in a local club. Sparks flew between the handsome crooner and the beautiful young lady in the audience. They fell in love and she married him, escaping the life she had at home. Shortly after the wedding, they moved to Los Angeles, where Daddy pursued his singing career. While he sang and made recordings, Mama took a job in the office of a factory to help support them.

It was during this time that my older brother, Robert, was born in 1943, at Children's Hospital in Los Angeles. When his right lung collapsed shortly after birth, he became the first baby in medical history to survive lung surgery, which earned him the nickname "Lucky."

Mama told me later that Daddy sang in the chorus behind Bing Crosby, whose hit song "White Christmas" was played every year around the holidays, always going to the top of the charts. When Daddy performed at nightclubs, it meant late nights and beautiful women in the audience. Unable to resist some of the women, he began to stray. When Mama found out about his affairs, she took Lucky, jumped on a train to Meadville, and didn't look back. Daddy quickly followed, and I don't believe he ever strayed again.

Whether he enlisted or was drafted into the Army really doesn't matter. Daddy returned home from World War II with a bad rash on his body that never went away, and a scrapbook of pictures that showed the horrors of war in Germany. His service as a professional photographer made me wonder how his sensitive nature survived.

Back in Meadville, Daddy took a job at the local newspaper, *The Meadville Tribune*. He worked as a photographer for the paper as well as a writer with the editorial staff.

∷

Daddy came to the hospital the night I was born. When he looked at me, as if there could be no doubt, he said, "She looks exactly like me." I became the apple of his eye, his favorite. After my birth I was brought home to a house on Lord Street, built in the late 1800s. A white wooden porch wrapped around the front of the house and the large side yard led to the garage for our car. My brothers and I slept in the attic under the eaves and near the large windows. Our family rented half of this house and another family rented the other half.

When I was two years old, brother Donnie arrived. I crawled upstairs where he was in his crib wrapped in blankets. I pinched him hard, made him cry, then quickly toddled off to another room, never to be caught. Sometimes I took down my panties and pooped behind the drapes to show my extreme dislike for this new person in the household. Yet Donnie became my best friend and constant playmate. He took good directions from me in his early years. He even ate dirt that I fed him from a teaspoon. Sitting side by side in the driveway, I fiendishly said, "Eat this, Donnie, it's good for you." Mama, watching from the kitchen window, quickly put a stop to it. A few years later, I quit teasing him. Something I said sparked his fierce temper, and grabbing a large knife from the kitchen he chased me round and round the dining room table. I knew if he caught me, he would really hurt me.

When I was six, we moved out of the house on Lord Street to our own house on North Street. The house had three bedrooms and one bathroom and cost $14,000. Built into the side of a hill, it had many sets of stairs. Stairs went from the street to the front door, which led to a "Florida porch," a screened-in room with small, vertical windows called jalousies, with slats that cranked open and shut. A sofa swing couch, hung with metal chains, decorated the room, leaving space for bicycles and outside toys.

Daddy brought home four hundred dollars a month. We spent twenty-five dollars a week on groceries, which included a twenty-five-cent bag of candy for the family to share. Mama hid the bag high in the kitchen cupboards but I always found it. Taking many pieces from the bag, I ate them under my bedcovers, flashlight in hand, reading comic books, which gave me great pleasure. I overheard Mama say, "But Don, I hid them way up in the cupboard." I was a strong and sturdy child, and great at climbing.

∷

Summer meant the local park, Shady Brook Park, so named for the brook that ran through it. Arms swinging and full of happiness, I left the house early in black shorts and a freshly washed and ironed white blouse, on my way to the park. Each day I made a new craft of pot holders or clay objects, and took the finished product home to Mama.

One lazy summer evening when I was eight, Daddy and I took our usual walk to the baseball field to watch the players practice. Sitting next to Daddy on the wooden bleachers and hearing the crack of the baseballs against the bats made me feel good. While walking back home, he let go of my hand. Leaning against a telephone pole, Daddy rested several minutes, not saying a word. Many minutes later he straightened up, put my hand in his, and we continued the walk home. I did not realize what happened but he had had a heart attack, his second. I don't know when he had his first. After this, Daddy was confined to his room while he recuperated. For some reason, Lucky, Donnie, and I were not allowed to see him.

∴∴

My first school was East End Elementary. I earned mostly As, with a few Bs, throughout the first six years. I was very shy, but always got the most Valentine cards, from both boys and girls. I had no idea why I was so well liked.

Susan Walker, the granddaughter of the founder of Talon Zippers, was my best friend throughout grade school. Our small wooden desks sat side by side in our classroom and we looked out the bank of windows that ran the length of the room, watching the seasons change. On the afternoons when I went to her house after school I saw a different world, one of a chauffeur, cook, and an upstairs and downstairs maid, as people who served were called in those days.

Susan was never allowed to come to my house, which was much more modest. Even though her parents sent me home in a chauffeured car, they would not let their daughter spend time in a neighborhood that wasn't as desirable as their own. When Susan's town car pulled up to our house, my brother Lucky would be waiting for me at the top of the stairs out front.

Lucky was a good older brother to me. He held my hand when we crossed the street, and in general looked after me. But his relationship with Mama was bad from the beginning. As a baby he would fling his feces out of his crib, and then fiendishly laugh when Mama had to clean everything. Lucky told me, "Mama spanked me too hard." He told me she took his model airplanes and threw them down the stairs, breaking them into little pieces. She laughed as she smashed his treasured planes that he had carefully glued and painted.

Often Lucky walked me to school, but one day he left before I did. I was walking alone when I saw a large boy, Joey Chase, walking on the other side of the street. He held sharp, jagged metal tops of soup cans that he tossed at my legs and ankles. Dressed in a frilly dress and white socks and shoes, I knew the tops would slice deeply, and draw blood. Growing furious, dropping my books and running across the street, I jumped on Joey and he fell to the sidewalk. I punched him first in the face, then on his stomach as hard as I could. I called him names until he cried. Other kids came along and I stopped, leaving him there. Continuing to school, I told my teacher. She sent me to the principal's office, where I told what had happened, then returned to class. They told me they would call my parents.

Daddy liked dinner served promptly at six o'clock. Seated in the massive, heavy furniture that our ancestors had brought with them on the ship when they came to America, dinner was a formal affair. Our dinner conversations were usually small talk about our day. But that night at dinner, the talk was about my incident at school. My parents weren't upset with me, which didn't surprise me. Mama always encouraged me to have a fighting spirit.

"The principal's office called me about Diana," my mother told everyone. "I told him that Joey is bigger than she is. He was really trying to hurt her."

"Calm down, E. J. It's over," was all Daddy said.

But there was input from our dog as she lay at our feet under the table. Duchess, a beautiful boxer dog, once caught a rat in midair, killing it when the rat jumped at Mama as she was doing laundry in the basement. Duchess could do no wrong after that. She became very old, expelling putrid-smelling farts that made us children laugh, Mama laughing loudest of all.

The spring rainy season came, making the sidewalk cement smell warm as we slipped through the raindrops, kicking the puddles, trying to get home fast. "Clap!" went the lightning that lit up the sky. Then we counted the seconds before the next boom of thunder. The number of seconds told us how far away the lightning was, as we hurried home to read Nancy Drew and the Hardy Boys books.

One rainy afternoon, Mama told me I had been born in the magic woods, under the leaves of wonderful flowers in the land of fairies and leprechauns. This made me feel loved and special. Of course, I believed her.

When it rained, we spent a lot of time indoors.

My most vivid memory of the house was the smell of food. There was always something wonderful on the stove. Mama made breakfast, lunch, dinner and all holiday meals in this kitchen. I thought she was the best cook in the whole world.

The milkman made deliveries to the back door. The glass milk bottles had a hard paper top with a wire to hold the paper. As she knelt beside me, I watched as Mama unscrewed the wire and dipped a spoon into the bottle to get the pure cream on the top. "Hmmm, that's good," Mama said, licking her lips before giving me a taste.

On weekends, Mama cooked fried eggs with sausage or bacon in a big cast iron skillet. She made biscuits from scratch served with real butter, or waffles, made in a heavy steel wafflemaker. Pancakes or oatmeal with a side dish of warm prunes and raisins gave us energy for the day to come.

My favorite lunch was Campbell's tomato soup served with a grilled cheese sandwich made with Wonder Bread that came in a white plastic bag with red, yellow and blue dots. But when we had war staples, which were chipped beef that came in a small glass jar or spam that came in a can, both tasted like they were left over from the war.

Meat roasts smothered in onions and carrots and served with mashed potatoes and peas made Sunday dinner special. Daddy loved pie so a different pie, made from scratch, was served after every dinner.

Mama knew the part of Meadville settled by the Italians, and she learned to make spaghetti from them. She cooked the sauce until it came to a full boil and then let it simmer for a long afternoon with the spaghetti sauce smell wafting into each room in the house. Hamburger and pork, arriving in brown paper fresh from the butcher shop, was ground by Mama using a metal meat grinder attached by a vise to the edge of the kitchen counter.

"Let's see if the noodles stick against the wall," Mama said as she threw several strands. If they stuck, the spaghetti was done. Served with olives, peeled raw carrots, Italian bread from the bakery, and a preserve from the garden, it was delicious and we ate well.

She tried to teach me to cook. "Write down what I am doing," Mama said as she sat me down on a stool in the kitchen and gave me pencil and paper.

Because I need to learn by doing, this did not work, and I never learned to cook. Liking everything to be perfect, Mama did the laundry too, and I never learned that skill either. She did tell me that when I was old enough to vacuum, I should do the cleaning in high heels and a short skirt. This advice served me well later in life.

My parents were strict. After a bath, we came downstairs in our pajamas, said good night, went to bed and that was it. But I knew my parents loved me. I felt it. And they loved each other. Every day, before Daddy came home for lunch, Mama would freshen her makeup. After lunch they would go to the bedroom to take a nap. Sometimes Daddy lovingly patted my mother's behind when he passed behind her. I knew this meant he loved her.

Our family had very little contact with our extended family in Meadville. Mama's aunt who was her adoptive mother was the only one allowed to visit, which she did often. Her name was Irene Magdalene First and we laughed at her initials of "I.M. First." The name of her husband, Mama's adopted father, was never mentioned.

"Irene is coming for a visit," Mama told us. Gram, as we children always called her, brought gum, comic books, and lots of candy. She loved to cook, and the meals were always just a little bit better when she was there.

I never knew where Gram lived because she had a job with the R.L. Polk Company. This company took the census, counting people in the United States manually. Gram went from town to town, walking door-to-door and asking people questions about their family.

Gram slept in my bed when she visited. When I was seven years old, she unbuttoned the top buttons of her nightgown and put my hands on her bare breasts. I felt very strange. Taking my hands away, I rolled over, putting my back to her. Nothing was said in the morning. She never did it again.

I wasn't afraid of Gram, but I began to fear Mama's anger. Anything could trigger it. Once when I was taking a bath and having a good time playing with my pink bubble gum by pulling it apart and sticking pieces on the bathtub faucet, Mama entered the room and saw the gum.

"What have you done, Diana?" she screamed.

Then she yanked me by the arm and pulled me out of the tub. I was naked and dripping wet when she spanked my butt with a big flat wooden hairbrush. More than the spanking, I remember the terror of knowing it was coming. She sat me down in front of the mirror, looked at me, and said, "You will never be pretty," which were scarring words to a young girl's soul.

I knew better than to tell Daddy.

Mama separated the family not only physically but verbally. Fixing my hair for school, she yanked on my ponytail very hard, saying about whatever little thing I had done wrong, "You didn't get that bad habit from my side of the family. That came from your father's side."

I wrote in my diary that I did not want her for a mother. She read my diary and for many months acted like the feeling was mutual.

But I loved her fiercely. Watching a TV show called *I Remember Mama* made me realize that someday she would die and that thought made my heart hurt most of all.

Fall brought with it the changing of the brilliantly colored leaves with the colors going into their veins. Robert raked the bundles of leaves, sweeping them to the curb by the street and making a big pile to be burned after dinner. Smelling the burning leaves in the crisp autumn air gave a final end to summer, paving the way for the crispness of a new year.

Lucky asked us to call him by his given name, Robert. It took practice, but we learned to do so. Robert was twelve when I heard the grown-ups, gathered in the living room, talking quietly, a bit of fear in their voices. Robert had made a fire in the football stadium across from us, one large enough for the fire trucks to come. Probably due to Daddy's status in the community, he did not get into trouble with the police. All was not as well in the Essig household as it appeared to the outside world.

"We are getting a television set!" Mama excitedly exclaimed.

The mid-1950s television received three network stations, CBS, NBC, and ABC. We watched *I Love Lucy*, *The Ed Sullivan Show*, and *The Lawrence Welk Show* with eager anticipation. Daddy sat on the couch, Mama in a chair, and Robert, Donnie, and I lay on the carpeted floor, perched on our elbows. Mama would slip out of her chair, go to the kitchen, and whip up eclairs, fudge, or brownies.

"We can't stay up too late, because tomorrow we are going on a special outing," Daddy told us one evening.

Getting up early, Mama packed our picnic basket and, while driving to Niagara Falls, we sang songs along the way. When we arrived we walked through the tourist store, where I saw a jackknife with a colored picture of the falls painted on the outside.

"Please, oh please, Daddy, can I have it?" I begged. Against Mama's wishes, he bought it for me. Back in the car, in the backseat with Robert and Donnie, I snapped the blade shut over my middle finger, almost cutting it off.

More afraid of Mama than of getting blood all over the car upholstery, I held my bleeding finger with my other hand, trying to keep the blood from escaping.

Soon it was all over the backseat and floor of the car. Both brothers looked at me silently with frightened eyes. Robert finally spoke up. The drive to the hospital seemed to take forever. I almost lost the middle finger on my left hand.

Mama wasn't angry with me, which surprised me. I learned that when I needed her, she took control and handled the situation.

The next day was Sunday, and on Sundays, without fail and on every religious holiday, we went to High Mass at Saint Brigid Roman Catholic Church. Through my child's eyes this church was as grand as any in Rome, massively built and beautiful with rich wooden pews and sunlit stained-glass windows. Smelling the burning incense during the Mass, said in Latin, gave an air of mystic worship and a feeling of closeness to God.

We wore our Sunday best which included special Sunday shoes, and hats and short white gloves for Mama and me. During church services Daddy would genuflect as he left our pew, going to the back of the church to climb the winding spiral staircase that led to the choir section. My heart felt like it would burst and my spine got tingles when his pure clear tenor voice soared and reached to the rafters as he sang "Ave Maria" without accompaniment.

On Sunday afternoons Daddy lay on the couch in either his green or gray sweater, both of which smelled like him, and watched the football games. Cigarette smoke filled the living room air as his ashtray overflowed with butts from his unfiltered Lucky Strikes. Hearing the click of Daddy's Zippo lighter, the sound of the game, and the announcer's voice floating through the house, we knew all was right with the world.

My only childhood ambition was to be a nun, which my father squashed immediately. When I told the family my hopes over dinner, he said, "Well, why don't you wait a while and then think about it."

Daddy and Mama passed a look between them that said how horrible they thought a life with no family, no children, and no social life would be. It was not brought up again. The desire persisted for quite a while, then gradually faded.

::
::

The bitter cold winds of northern Pennsylvania, blowing over Lake Erie, brought winter in with a blast of ice and snow. After school, bundled into warm playsuits, we dragged our wooden sleds to the hill, going up and down, finding delight and newness as only children can when doing the same thing over and over.

"Leave your wet clothes and your ice skates in the Florida porch," Mama told us. "I will have the hot chocolate ready when you are out of the bath," she said. "Tomorrow you can make a snowman."

Christmas holiday movies from the 1950s could have been made at our house. Riding in the car at night, white cold in the air, we went to the Christmas tree lot outside of town and walked up and down the rows of trees to pick the perfect, round tree. Once found, it would be tied to the roof of the car for the drive home.

Magically, the next morning it was in our living room, the smell of the freshly cut cypress tree going to each room in the house, telling us it was Christmas.

The presents under the tree were wrapped so beautifully, but I just had to know what my presents were. Waking up in the early hours, warm in my red-footed sleeper, I carefully unwrapped all the presents meant for me. Then, I wrapped them back up. Mama finally got wise when, one year, I did not act surprised enough upon opening them.

She said, "Don, I am tired of paying for Christmas through July. We have to cut back next year." I figured out there was no Santa Claus and promptly told Donnie.

As I got older, many nights Daddy would return home from work, sit in the living room, and hold his head in his hands as if he had a big headache, and I knew he had problems he could not solve.

Daddy's illness had been hard on all of us. Although he was well liked at the *Tribune*, the paper couldn't hold his position indefinitely. The owner's son took over Daddy's job, making our future uncertain. Our savings wouldn't last for long so my parents tried to find a new way to support us.

Mama and Daddy answered an ad in the paper that promised you could make big money in the business of Cycle Massage chairs. Two representatives sat at the dining room table with them, painting a rosy picture of the massage chair business. Once you bought one of their franchises, you were sure to make great sums of money by selling these wonderful chairs. Their pitch was smooth and enticing. By the end of the evening, my parents made a decision that changed our lives. They took some of their savings and bought into a franchise.

"We're moving to West Lafayette, Indiana," Mama told us. "Daddy and I are setting up a business there."

Our family roots of one hundred and fifty years in Meadville were torn up. Six generations of our family had lived there and we were leaving the only town I had ever known, to travel to the unfamiliar land of Indiana.

My parents sold our house. We left our china, furniture, and most of our toys with friends and relatives. Mama had taught us to be strong. We faced the unknown together as a family.

::
::

Life in West Lafayette was a struggle for my parents. Mama went to work selling massage chairs, giving foot massages to potential buyers as a sales promotion. Daddy would go with her to the store where she demonstrated the chairs, probably to protect her from the men she encountered. "I am tired of massaging dirty, stinky feet," Mama said at night. Only occasionally did she sell a massage chair. It was dismal work that didn't support us. Mama and Daddy found out the salesmen who sold my parents the franchise had lied to them about the territory. Others had worked this area previously in the same business, making their franchise worthless.

We stayed in West Lafayette for about a year. The old familiar smells of Mama's cooking were gone. Driving home one night, Robert, Donnie, and I talked about dinner in the backseat of the car. "I guess we can have canned spaghetti," Mama said. It was her wooden tone of despair more than her words that told me the situation we were in.

Unlike my parents, I was thriving. I was a cheerleader at my new school, very popular and making good grades. One day, I was drinking water at the water fountain when I looked up and saw the principal standing over me.

"I want to meet the new girl who has taken this school by storm," he said.

What an impression that made on me. The principal, a man of great importance, had taken the time to come out of his office to meet me, making me feel important too.

Just as I was beginning to feel like I belonged, our lives were uprooted again. Unable to make a living, and facing the winter, we packed and moved to Orlando, Florida, where Mama had a great aunt and uncle she had never met. That was our only family connection, weak at best.

These were the years of my childhood each blending into the next. They gave me a good foundation to withstand the horrors that were to come.

Mama

Daddy

House in Meadville

First Communion

Gram

Easter Sunday

Lucky, Myself and Donnie

Daddy, Mama and Lucky

Chapter Two

YOUTH

Our family drove from Indiana to Orlando, Florida, in the winter of 1959, staying each night at a Howard Johnson motel. Robert joked that the motel chain must pipe the food from one location to the next, as all the meals tasted the same and the rooms were exactly alike.

Disney World, the real beginning of Orlando, would not come into being until 1971. The Orlando we encountered was vastly different from the theme park it would become.

Orange groves surrounded the city and the rich perfumed smell of their blossoms hung like a blanket, covering the warm summer nights. The scent from magnolia trees competed with orange blossoms but, not winning, blended in to make a powerful, wonderful smell that moved with the breeze in the soft summer nights.

During the day it was hot and the sun was brutal. When the rains came, the water poured down in torrents and sheets sometimes for days at a time. After a quick shower, the sun would magically appear, usually with a rainbow, but then the awful heat began again.

My parents had rented a small house in an area that had no trees and no azaleas called Azalea Park. The house, on Randia Drive, did not have air conditioning and was made of cinder blocks, not wood. It felt like a huge come-down from our home in Pennsylvania.

"Keep the windows open so a breeze will come in," Mama said after she, Daddy, and Robert painted the walls of each room in this small, three-bedroom house, causing us to breathe the fresh paint smell for weeks to come.

Our living room was sparsely furnished with two cane chairs and a Bahama couch made of cheap, fuzzy, beige material. It was clean, but not comfortable. Gray linoleum squares covered the floor of every room, with a green throw rug covering a portion of the living room floor. There was no dining room. We ate in the kitchenette using the small Formica table and chairs which we brought from Meadville.

The front yard was covered with crabgrass that felt like small ropes under my bare feet and the lack of trees made playing in the yard rough.

Huge palmetto bugs that looked like giant roaches flew into my bedroom at night. They sounded like small airplanes circling around trying to pick me up. "Ewww," I said to myself as I ducked under the covers to avoid them. I held my breath for as long as I could and then came up for air. Finally, I fell asleep. In the morning I shook my shoes to make sure no bugs had spent the night there.

"Orlando, Land of a Thousand Lakes" meant living near lakes that had a lot of snakes and alligators. When Robert, Donnie, and

I walked to a friend's house, the sand and swampland squished between our toes and through our thongs.

"Alligators can only see straight ahead so if a gator comes after you, zigzag when you run, Diana," Robert called out to me.

But the walks to school, like the days spent there, were uneventful. Colonial High School contained seventh through twelfth grade. The long, gray one-story building had open walkways, and the wind blew sand on us as we walked to and from classrooms whose windows remained open to catch any air. It felt barbaric to me. My grades began falling, reflecting my home life.

Our distant relatives, Great Aunt Martha and Uncle Ed, lived in a better part of Orlando. Their house was made of wood and the yard had real grass. When we went to visit, it felt like a different country. Spanish moss hung from the trees, giving the air a delicious ghost-like atmosphere, and the nearby swampland gave the area a musty smell. Some things stayed the same in our new house. I never went into Mama and Daddy's bedroom. Years before, I'd smeared lipstick all over Mama's lingerie and because of this I was forbidden from ever going into their bedroom again. An exception was made when Mama called me into the bedroom to explain how sex worked. Seated at her vanity, she used a tube of lipstick to represent the sexual organs of the male entering the female. But the "no entry" to their bedroom rule still applied.

Other things changed. Mama started sleeping late. Meals were no longer carefully prepared. Breakfast was whatever we could make for ourselves and we ate lunch at school. Dinner was something cheap and easy to fix.

On Saturdays, a ride to the airport to watch the airplanes land and take off and see the passengers pick up their luggage from the long, wooden conveyer belt became an occasional family outing.

Taking a drive around the city to see the lakes became another, but the outings soon faded.

Life was hard for Daddy. Considered an old man at age forty-seven, he could not get a job. Leaving early in the morning to look for work, he returned at night to sit in one of the cane chairs in the living room.

Once Mama said, sobbing, "Don, I can't go on like this. If you don't find a job, I will take the kids and go home."

Practical me thought, "Well, how will you do that?" We didn't have any money. We didn't have the fifty cents that the school required us to spend on our gym shorts. I felt the shame of no money and hard times.

We attended a small nearby church named Good Shepherd. Our Sunday church days, once a confirmed ritual, became sporadic, with Mama sometimes not going at all. Upon returning home after mass one Sunday, I slammed the flimsy screen door behind me and yelled at Daddy, "I will never go to church again." They were words I would regret for the rest of my life.

Shortly after my tantrum, Daddy left for a few days to drive to Tallahassee to look for a job. He was hired by a newspaper and then he made the long drive back, arriving too late to say goodnight to us children.

∴∴

It was April 2, 1960, and I was twelve. Gram was visiting and that night I heard the ambulance arrive with all its sirens, taking Daddy away. Hearing the car doors slam as Mama and Gram drove to the hospital that was clear across town, I drifted back to sleep.

Hours passed. I awoke to hear Mama and Gram talking in the living room. "Cold and alone. They wheeled him to a corner and left him there to die like a poor person, cold and alone," I heard Mama say.

Mama cried and cried, telling Gram that Daddy had climaxed while on top of her saying, "The flowers, the flowers, it is so beautiful here," and then began having terrible chest pains, which became his final heart attack.

I realized that Daddy had died.

The shock of Daddy's death had a surreal effect on me.

Lying in my bed, I had an out-of-body experience. Elevating, I felt I was floating in the air above my bed. I looked around the room and saw my body below me. I wasn't afraid but I didn't understand what was happening. In a few minutes I returned to my body and went back to sleep.

The next day, the family was busy getting ready for Daddy's funeral in Pennsylvania. Gram took me downtown to shop for a dress to wear to his funeral. "She does not look good in black," the saleswoman said to Gram. So Gram chose a dark brown checkered dress for me.

After shopping, we walked along the sidewalk. I looked up at the blue Florida sky, expecting to see Daddy's face behind a cloud, looking down at me. I knew he was in Heaven, somewhere up there behind the white pillow-like clouds. I kept searching and searching to find his face. The grief felt like a mountain of weight inside my chest.

I wore my new dress when we flew to Meadville for Daddy's funeral. The practice of the day was to have a wake in a house with the body lying in one room, ready for burial. Many people, most of them grown-ups, walked around the first floor of the house, eating and talking in hushed tones. Sliding among the adults, I walked quietly upstairs into the dark room where my father was laid out—the term for a body prepared for burial—in his open casket. At child's height I could not see his face, but standing on tiptoe I saw that he was dressed in his new gray pinstriped suit, his hands folded across his chest. Touching his finger, I jerked my finger back. It felt like a stick of wax. Quickly leaving the room I pressed through the adults and made my way outside. I started walking, thinking, "Gee, this is a narrow sidewalk." I was too numb to process thoughts of the reality.

The church taught us that death meant Heaven or Hell but I knew that death meant he was never coming back. The funeral was held at Saint Brigid Church. Daddy's open casket was on display in front of the altar.

Accompanied by organ music and paired as couples, Mama and Donnie, Robert and I, walked from the back down the long aisle of the church. I consciously willed my inner composure to take over so my grief would not show on my face.

Finally, reaching the first pew in front of the casket, we genuflected and took our seats. Mass was said along with a memorial to Daddy. Then the casket was firmly shut. We left, riding in a black limousine, the first car in a procession of many, for the drive to the cemetery. Later I learned there were over four hundred people at the funeral. It made me feel good to think that so many people liked my father.

We returned to Orlando, and Gram left a few days later. In the coming weeks Mama took a rocking chair and put it outside the hallway to the bedroom. She would not go into the bedroom, and her hair turned white over the next month when she was sitting there, rocking in that chair. I came home from school, looked at the chair, looked at her, and then went past her to my room.

Once, when she was gone and the house was empty, I stood in the doorway of Mama and Daddy's bedroom and looked at the bed, all neatly made, thinking, *So this is where Daddy died.* But no one talked about anything. We never did talk about feelings.

∴

Daddy left a small blue notebook. In it, in his beautiful handwriting, he started a letter that said:

Robert-Diana-Donnie,

Below are the things I would learn to do (if I were you) in order to live a happy normal life. It is very hard for me to express in words the things I know so well in my mind. The only way for me to do this is to just dive in and say which of the requisites come first into my mind.

First, of course, comes religion. I do not believe you can be truly happy without worshipping God.

Next in importance is your relationship with the people who will be around you all your life. This is most important because no one is self-sufficient. All your life you will either be doing things for people or they will be doing things for you. The degree in which you can adjust yourself to different kinds of people will determine to a marked degree your success in life.

Remember that there isn't a person in the world that does not have a flaw in his character, a fault in his or her makeup.

And the letter ends there as if he meant to finish it. Mama saved it and now I keep it in a safety deposit box in an envelope that says, "From Daddy."

He left an insurance policy and Mama used the money to buy a house around the corner on Dahlia Drive. This house too had no air conditioning, or if it did, Mama never ran it.

She kept us on a strict budget. "The tub can only have two inches of water," Mama told us as we prepared to take a bath. It took gas to heat the water and that cost money. She required "military" showers, which meant turning on the water to get wet, turning off the water, soaping down, and then turning the water on again for a fast rinse-off.

Mama was still beautiful. Her only skills were that of being a wife and mother, so she found it hard to get a job. She often asked us, "What man would want a woman with three teenage children?" which made me feel terrible.

In order to support us, Mama worked hard and got her real estate license. But it was a man's world. The bosses made her drive long hours to sit and look pretty at housing development showings that offered little chance for her to make a sale. But she was a hard worker and she tried.

Mama never complained as she scrimped and saved so the four of us could have a summer pass to the local swimming pool. This was great for me and I lived in my black tank swimsuit, putting it on first thing in the morning and taking it off last thing at night, always slightly smelling of chlorine. A tight white swim cap completed the ensemble.

I loved to swim and dive and was good at it. Trained professional divers from Germany saw me dive and came to the house to talk with Mama. They wanted to take me back to Germany to train but Mama said no. She did not know them and was afraid something bad would happen to me.

There were tender moments with Mama. For my birthday, she took me to a wholesale jewelry store. I saw a beautiful gold ring with a single pearl on it. Mama asked the salesperson the price. "Eleven dollars," the clerk said. I saw Mama's face tighten. "Can we afford it?" I asked, looking up at her. "Yes," she said. I knew I would treasure that ring forever.

All of us were adjusting to life without Daddy. Mama was depressed. She began sleeping a lot. We were all careful not to make any noise that might disturb her. I did not want to hear, "Let me sleep. What are you doing, for God's sake let me sleep," coming in yells and screams. It was as if her return to reality was hell.

I started to smoke when I was thirteen, taught by a girlfriend who smoked Winston cigarettes. Mama smoked and let me smoke at home. I felt this was wrong, I should not be smoking at home but Robert smoked too and so I continued. In later years, a three-pack-a-day smoker, I would put a lit cigarette in an ashtray, take a shower, get out, and continue smoking the cigarette. Putting that one out, I lit another, developing a nasty habit that would last thirty-five years.

∷

Every woman remembers when and how she lost her virginity. In my fourteenth summer, David McGiven, a friend from school who was a few years older, asked me to ride with him in the backseat of his car. I said yes. The driver, David's older brother, had his girlfriend in the front seat with him. He suggested that the four of us go to his parents' house. The fact that the house was in a very nice neighborhood impressed me and I murmured a response that I wanted to go.

Arriving at David's house, we quickly went to his parents' bedroom, lay on top of the bedspread and had fumbling teenage sex. After a hurried entry into me, David pulled out, left a skinny stream of cum, and then we got up. It was not the best way to find out about sex, but not the worst either.

Sexual stirrings of primitive desires came to me when I listened to the music of the sixties, rock and roll. Mama bought me a small, silver transistor radio that I treasured. "Everybody Loves Somebody Sometime," sang Dean Martin. "Are you Lonesome Tonight?," an Elvis song, played in my daydreams. Playing the music as often as I could during the day, and beneath my pillow at night, I heard love stories and the promise of a boyfriend to come.

When a friend of my brother Robert's asked me to go to the drive-in movies, I was happy to go. Richard and I had sex in the backseat of his car that night, and several times later. The sex was better than the first time with David.

Mama started going out most nights, starting the evening with Donna, one of the few girlfriends she ever had. They began at Johnnie's, a local beer and wine place, and then moved on to the Villa Nova, a fancy restaurant that had dancing. She parked her car in the driveway instead of putting it in the garage, so I knew she was out most of the night. She never brought a man home, and made sure we did not know what had happened when she was gone. Years later, she told me she had been hooked on "black beauties"—uppers.

∴

The stage was ripe for me to become a victim of rape. My fifteenth birthday came and went in June. Walking home, wearing a white waitress uniform from the corner drugstore where I had a summer job serving the lunch counter, I felt a car drive up behind me.

Walking on the top of the curb, as a child does, balancing one foot in front of the other, I stopped when I recognized the driver of the new Cadillac. Top down, his tan arm resting on the side, Tex said, "Jump in, I'll take you the rest of the way home." I thought it was perfectly normal to accept a ride home, as he was one of the many friends who would come to the house and pick Mama up before taking her out to dinner.

We drove the few short blocks to the house. The next afternoon I found he had asked Mama if he could take me to Miami for a week to sightsee.

Mama kept saying, "They will have separate rooms," and "Diana will get to see the world, something I never did. Let's take a family vote and make a decision."

Gram was visiting, and Mama called all of us into the living room. We gathered in a circle and made the decision standing up. Taking about five minutes, with not much discussion, Gram and Robert voted a fast no. Donnie, who was swayed by Mama's and my yes votes, voted yes. This made it three to two, and the floor of my life was about to fall out from under me again.

Tex and I arrived in Miami at night at the first of what was to be many motel rooms. Tall, tan, and big, he stood near the bathroom saying, "Your mother told me it was okay to share a room. We need to save money."

Feeling blind terror, like a murder victim must feel, numbing shivers of fear traveled down my spine, into my back and through my stomach. The saving money part fit, but I knew I was in for it. I was five feet two inches tall and weighed a hundred pounds. I couldn't fight him.

Not knowing how I got there, curled up against the headboard of the bed, my feet dug into the mattress. I tried to push myself away from Tex. Knees held tightly against my chest, I curled into a ball, trying to make myself small and get out of reach of his big, hairy arms. When he crawled on top of me he looked so old and he smelled very old.

I remember looking down at the pillows, and realize now that I elevated out of my body for the second time in my life. My spirit left my body when life became too much to bear.

A rape victim can have little recall, and this is true for me. I don't remember sleeping or waking up or getting back into the next night's bed. He must have fed me, as I remember a blur of sitting across from him in a cheap soda jerk place, picking at my sandwich. I had been an obedient child and obeyed him. But in the hotel room, I must have screamed a lot because for the rest of the trip, each night we drove to a new motel.

Why didn't I call for help? I'm sure there was a phone in the room but I didn't know how to make a long-distance call with no money. More importantly, I did not think Mama had the money to get me home. I was constantly filled with fear. It paralyzed me.

One morning, while Tex was in the hotel room, I sat on the steps outside. Wearing my black shorts and a white blouse, I clutched the hot galvanized pipe railing as a man and a woman walked by. The woman was stooped over, as if from many years of work. She wore a multicolored bandana around her head. They looked like an immigrant couple, and it seemed they had been married many years. They must have been in a neighboring room and heard my screams the night before. "I think we should do something," the woman said. "No, just keep going," the man responded. That lesson stayed with me. I never ignore a situation where a person might be in distress.

Blocked out is the memory of the drive home with Tex or my arrival at the house. Once safe at home, I sat in the bathtub, in the required two inches of water. Mama stood in front of the bathroom medicine cabinet mirror, with her back to me, putting on her makeup. "Did you have a good time?" she asked. "Yes," I replied dully, not looking at my body. A few tears fell down my cheeks, but not many.

Tex did not come around much after that, and I never told Mama what happened. I knew she would find him and kill him. From that day on, my psychiatrist later told me, I had no parents.

∴

At the end of the summer, I began my sophomore year in high school. My anger at the world began coming out when I climbed to the ceiling by way of an open closet, and using a bright red marker wrote "Fuck You" so students could see it. Never doing any homework, I could usually pass a test with a decent grade. Just to make sure, I began cheating and did so even on my SATs.

When a student was absent, school authorities would call the parent to find out why. Not realizing it meant Mama could not get calls of her own, I undid the inside wires of our only phone, which was a pink Princess with a long cord that could be taken into each of our bedrooms. The phone would not ring all day until I reconnected it, giving me absolute freedom, and, unfortunately, no calls to Mama.

Arriving home late one afternoon, I put rollers in my hair and then began rewiring the phone so it would ring. Mama came out of her bedroom, saw what I was doing, and in a raised voice asked, "What are you doing? Where have you been? What time is it?"

"What business is it of yours?" came from me.

She smacked me across the face, hard. In return I smacked her across her face. It hurt when she grabbed the hair rollers in my hair and began pulling. She was stronger and bigger and I immediately backed off.

By the third year of high school I was skipping many school days. Cruising around with my girlfriends in their car, we went to the drive-in restaurant called Steak and Shake. Cruising turned into trips to Daytona Beach, where, in the fancy hotels that had coins in the fountains, I nimbly collected enough for food and gas.

My self-esteem was slipping away, and I thought having sex with the boys who were popular in school would make me more popular. When a boy called me on the telephone, I arranged to meet him nearby, in his car.

The captain of our football team was obsessed with taking girls' virginity. Once he had scored, he would give his varsity jacket to his latest trophy so she could wear it at school and everyone would know his latest conquest. He asked me if I was a virgin. After he found out I had lied, he took back his infamous jacket and left.

Several times, late at night, a car full of boys drove up our driveway, over the grass and stopped in front of my bedroom window, then hollered, "Whore! Whore!" as they drove across the front of the house, then over the curb onto the next street. The feeling of shame overcame me.

I did not go to any dances at school because I was never asked. I wanted to crawl into a shell on the nights of the prom and other big dances. Mama never seemed to notice.

She taught me to drive and I got my license.

Mama was dating a man named Doc, a nice, jovial man who dressed well even though he did not have a regular job. He contributed money to the household, and occasionally slipped me a few dollars. So when I asked to borrow his 1949 Packard to drive my friends around, he replied with an easy yes. It did not take long before I had an accident that was my fault. Once again, it was not talked about.

I begged Mama to let me drive her car, a brand-new white Comet with red interior that she loved. One day while I was driving, Donnie was in the passenger seat eating a huge barrel of Kentucky Fried Chicken. He looked up and calmly said, "I think you're going to crash into the back of that truck." He said it twice before I did. I had the second accident that was my fault, which caused Mama's car insurance premiums to go sky-high. I had created a financial burden on her that I did not understand.

A few weeks later, I came home from school, walked into the living room, and saw Mama sitting in the round, pink chair sobbing. Drying bitter tears, Mama looked at me, and said, "I tried to get rid of you, to give you away, but no one will take you. I called the police and the church and I don't know what to do with you." My heart cracked into pieces as I walked to my bedroom and shut the door.

Going wild, waking at midnight, I snuck out of the house, pushing Robert's car down the driveway. Popping it into gear to start the engine, I jumped in. I never got stopped as I drove around the city for hours, the radio turned up loud. Coasting into the driveway with the car engine turned off, I snuck back into the house.

I got a job. Taking the bus, I went to another part of town and worked afternoons after school and on Saturdays at a dress store called Diana Shops. I rang up sales, straightened clothes, and swept the floor. My boss, a woman, was strict, and I did well, giving Mama fifteen dollars a month for household expenses.

∴

In my fifteenth year the Vietnam War was escalating and Robert enlisted in the Air Force. He was sent to Denver to teach, and remained in Colorado after his discharge. Mama read his letters out loud to Donnie and to me. In one of his last letters he wrote that he had a bad motorcycle accident that crushed his right wrist and also his dreams of becoming a doctor. His letters became sparse as he explained he had chosen optometry as a profession.

Early one morning I stumbled over Donnie. Crouched outside Mama's door, his knees against his chest, he looked like he had been there a long time. When I asked him, "What are you doing?" he slowly replied, "Mom tried to kill herself last night so I took her gun." There was so little talking in the house I never followed up and asked him if he gave it back to her. But I'm sure he did.

By this time Mama was not cooking much, although she did slip Donnie a few dollars to go to the local drugstore for a hot meal or a sandwich. I have no idea where I ate, but there was always cereal and milk for breakfast, or peanut butter and jelly for a sandwich.

∴

As all girls know, the betrayal of a girlfriend, a best friend, can hurt like no other. When I was a junior, I was in a clique of five girls and I placed the ultimate value on our friendship. We would talk incessantly on the phone at night about boys, about school, about everything and nothing, each one calling another to see what had been said. At school we met in the hall, grouped together, and talked about the same thing we did the night before, then went home to get on the phone and talk some more.

We began stealing. One day after school, we took the bus to the local shopping mall to shoplift small items in the department store. One day we got caught. The manager of the store had all five of us get on the store escalator with him and directed us toward his office. One of us, Roxanne Blix, a straight-A student and cheerleader, had an excellent reputation at school. While we were on the escalator, Roxanne slipped a tube of mascara into my side pocket without my knowing it.

"Empty your purses and pockets. Put everything on the floor, directly in front of you," came the command from the manager. And there it was, the stolen tube of mascara, in my pocket.

"I did not steal the mascara," I told the manager. It did not matter.

I did not tell on Roxanne but when we were released from the store and walking home, the words flew among us, the girls saying, "Even if Roxanne did steal it, she has the most to lose at school because she could get a scholarship to college." The implication was I was not as good as Roxanne.

The clique completely ostracized me. Now I had no friends and no one to talk to on the phone at night or meet in the hallways at school. I was crushed and hurt as only a teenage girl can feel who loses her best friend and all her friends at once.

Doc, Mama's friend, knew how to take care of things like this. He went to the police station, came back and said, "It is all taken care of. There will be no charges against Diana." He had fixed things. This was my first lesson on the injustice of the justice system. After he stopped coming around, Mama told me that he was in the Miami "underground." She heard that he had been killed and buried in the concrete paving under the new highway.

Not only was I stealing small items, I began stealing clothes to wear. Mama tried to teach me to dress, using the colors of black and white as a base, but we went to inexpensive stores and it made me feel poor. Pulling on the deep anger inside me, I took a bus to the best department stores by myself. It was easier to steal that way.

"Where are you getting your clothes? I really like the blue dress with pocket zippers," came from Mama.

I answered, "There is a group at school that is selling fenced clothes." She asked if I could get her some clothes too. "I will put in the request," I replied.

Always happily surprised to pay little for top-notch clothes that somehow just suited her, she eventually grew suspicious. Even though this was good extra spending money for me, I stopped before she could question me further.

In my senior year I wanted to be Homecoming Queen. I went from student to student and asked them to vote for me. It was that simple, and the announcement came over the loudspeaker that I had won.

At a nearby payphone, I called Mama and told her the news, which made her very proud. I saw the school newspaper that said "Diana Essig, Homecoming Queen," but then in the space of a few hours it was recalled and Carol Kellam, a student who had contributed a lot to extra school activities, was announced as the new queen. It took me a few years to realize that Carol was the better representative of the school and the people in charge had changed the vote.

∷

In 1965, the summer of my eighteenth year, I graduated from high school. Walking to the stage to get my diploma, with

Mama and Donnie in the audience, all I wanted was to feel invisible. Getting a diploma meant nothing to me, and I felt there was nothing to be proud of. Even thought I had missed many days along with the entire last six weeks of my senior year, I had graduated.

By now Mama was at her wits' end. She called Daddy's sister, my Aunt Evelyn, to ask if I could spend the summer with her and her husband in Flemington, New Jersey. I could not remember ever meeting them. Evelyn said yes.

In New Jersey, I discovered that my aunt and uncle were strict disciplinarians. I respected them and became the model child, except that the job they had gotten for me in the cut-glass factory was at the cash register, and I was stealing. I hid the stolen bills in my travel bag when I went home after work. The rest of the time was spent as a family. Each evening, I brought the newspaper in from the yard to Uncle Dick and helped Aunt Evelyn prepare meals. We had a routine. Movies, a play at a local theater, and an introduction to a nice young boy completed this new way of life.

I obeyed all the rules. Aunt Evelyn answered Mama's telephone questions saying, "Of course, she is fine. We really enjoy having her here." I don't think they ever found out about the stealing. When Aunt Evelyn, who worked for a travel agency, wanted to take a trip around the world, I was sent home.

Living back under the same roof with Mama, I reverted to my old ways, going out, drinking, using a false ID to enter clubs, and coming home late.

Returning very late one night, I unlocked the bottom lock on the front door and tried to open it but discovered Mama had put a new lock on the inside with a security chain on it. With my small hands, I reached around the partially opened door and slid the chain off. The noise awakened her. When I opened the door, she flicked on the lights. There she stood, naked, with a gun in her hand. I got hysterical with laughter.

Losing her temper, she angrily pushed me out the front door. Going to my room, she screamed at the top of her lungs, "Get out! Get out and stay out!" She threw my clothes onto the front yard, and then locked the front door again when she was finished, chain bolt and all.

I slept in her car that night. The next morning I took the bus to an apartment where many girls lived. I knew one of them and the rest agreed I could move in. Joining in their late-night parties with liquor, random sex became routine.

Again I got a job, going to work full-time at an insurance company processing claims. Not realizing the effect I had on the people's lives I was reviewing, I followed a formula, checking boxes to show if the person on paper would receive insurance benefits.

Able to enroll in college tuition-free because of Daddy's service in the war, I enrolled in Orlando Jr. College for night classes. There I met a tall, dark, handsome young man named Bill Mead. "Come to my house. It's across the street," Bill said to me. "My mother's not home." Between classes, he taught me how to give a blow job.

Saturdays, at Daytona Beach, I always looked for Bill. Seeing him standing on the sand talking with two stunning blonde women, I went over and he introduced them to me as Carol and Mary Young. Later he told me that they were high class hookers, known as the Young Sisters. Carol would play a big part in my future.

Sex in the daytime, sex at night. I got pregnant.

Daddy

Family on Dahlia Drive

Mama

Robert

Donnie

High School Days

Gram

Painting of Mama

Mama and Doc

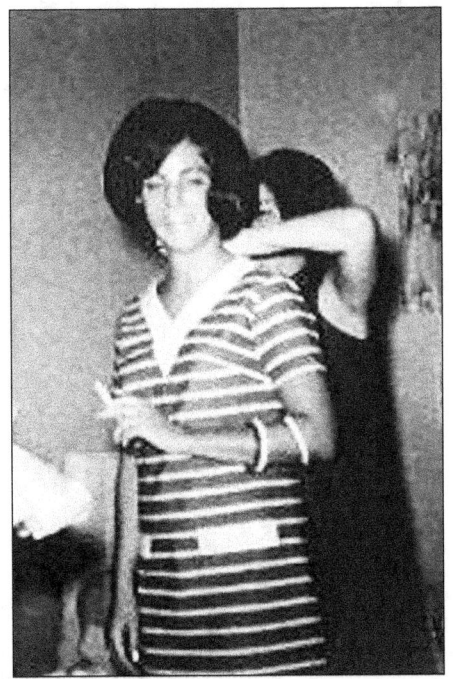
Getting Ready to Go Out

Family

Chapter Three

THE BABY AND PROSTITUTION

When an unmarried girl got pregnant in the 1960s, people whispered and gossiped about her. She would be whisked away to stay with relatives or friends until the baby was born. When she returned, only her best friends were told a few secrets. It was all very mysterious.

When I got pregnant, I had no idea what would happen to my baby and me. I had violent morning sickness constantly. Standing near the bus stop to go to work, I threw up all over the nearest tree. I knew I had to tell Mama so I decided to visit her. The night before, for the first time in my life, I could not go to sleep.

The morning brought a beautiful Florida winter day. I walked up to the house and found Mama sitting in the round pink chair in the living room. She looked at me as if she already knew I was in some kind of trouble.

When I said simply, "I'm pregnant," Mama did not ask questions.

"You may move back into your room," she told me.

Within a week, she took me to Catholic Charities, a support group of the Catholic Church that helped unwed mothers. Questions were asked about my sex life as I was interviewed and counseled to give the baby up for adoption. A few weeks later Mama drove me to a home for unwed mothers in Port Orange, a small dusty town near Tampa and a two-hour drive from Orlando.

Before leaving, Mama took me shopping for material for my maternity clothes, which she would sew for me.

"Choose carefully because we can only afford two dresses and they will have to last you."

I did not listen and chose heavy, cheap muslin fabric, one blue and white striped and the other yellow and white striped. I am sure that Mama shed many bitter tears while she sewed them for me. Having loved my father very much, she must have felt that she had failed him. I wore those two hot, uncomfortable dresses and a pair of thongs for the remainder of my pregnancy.

∴

"The Home" was the house of a middle-aged couple who were paid to take in unwed girls. There were six of us girls living there and we were all close in age and due to deliver at about the same time.

Seldom talking at the dining room table, we spoke more freely when we were in our room sitting on our beds. Not having much family life, I did not join in when the girls spoke of their relatives. But when the girls spoke about their baby's father, I spoke up. I did not know for certain who fathered my child but I secretly hoped it was Bill Mead. I talked of how handsome he was.

Our only time to leave the house was on Sunday morning when we went to church. Marching single file down the aisle, we could feel the eyes of the parishioners on us, judging us girls of ill repute.

No education or information was given to us about our pregnancies or what to expect with the upcoming birth. When I felt a sack of extra skin by my anus, I thought it was extra skin being made for the baby. I found out later it was hemorrhoids. I began to feel the baby, to feel his soul. It felt heavy, psychologically very heavy.

At the time it was normal to gain quite a bit of weight when having a baby. I always asked for second helpings at the dining table. On my birthday, I ate many pieces of chocolate cake. My two Empire-style dresses had left ample room for weight gain. I gradually reached 192 pounds.

We girls were taken to a clinic where we saw a doctor who examined us and estimated our time of delivery.

"My weight in high school was 110 pounds," I told the nurse. Her throaty reply was a deep "Hmmmm," as if she did not believe me. I got no exercise and had gained eighty pounds. By my calculations I was a month overdue. I was huge.

It was hard for Mama to come and see me. She had taken another job in the real estate business working long hours, trying to make a living. Once, when she picked me up to go for a fish dinner, she looked at my legs and said, "You've lost your knees, you don't have knees anymore."

My legs looked like tree stumps, I had gained so much weight. After an uncomfortable dinner, Mama had to leave for the two-hour drive back.

OFF MY KNEES

∷

On August 30, 1966, two months after my nineteenth birthday, I was taken to the hospital, and labor was induced. Painkillers were not allowed with induced labor. I had no one to intervene for me. Mama did not arrive until I was giving birth.

I was screaming loudly and swearing profusely when I heard the bars on each side of my bed lift and lock into place. Then the nurse pushed my bed into a small empty room and left me by myself. Cursing, I tried to bend the steel bars on the side of the bed as an outlet for my pain.

The nurse occasionally popped her head in, but she never entered the room. Finally, after many hours she came in, then pushed my bed to the delivery room. Mama was sitting on a stool and stood up as my bed rolled next to her. Then the wheels clicked and the bed was locked firmly in place again.

Squeezing the bars, and holding Mama's hand, I pushed and pushed, starting to deliver. I wondered if my child was resisting being born, not wanting to come into the world to face the life he was about to live. I saw the top part of the baby's head come out. Then I lost consciousness.

My baby was a boy. He was extremely large, one inch longer than my womb. "I don't know how she carried him," the doctor remarked. That confirmed my thoughts that, as a charity patient, I had not received the best of care.

I awoke to find myself in a room with other unwed mothers, our beds lined up in a row. We could hear the newborn babies crying from a nearby room. Unlike the married mothers, we were not allowed to see our newborns.

The same nurse who had wheeled me screaming and cursing into the delivery room now looked down at me. "Tsk, tsk, tsk, and I thought you was a lady," she said, putting a rueful smile on my face.

On my visits with the social worker from Catholic Charities, she told me each time not to look at my baby after he was born because it would be too hard to give him up, so I did not. But Mama did, saying he was the most beautiful baby she had ever seen. "Are you sure you want to sign the papers and give the baby away?" she asked me. "Yes," I said, knowing I could never raise him or give him any kind of a life. The papers were brought to me soon after delivery, when I was still in the hospital. I signed them, thinking I would give him up for adoption, and that would be that.

My baby was sent to an interim home to wait for his adoption. Each new baby was named alphabetically with the next letter. "G" was the next one up, so he became "Baby George" until he was adopted.

∴

After the delivery, I went back to live with Mama on Dahlia Drive. She bought me a rubber Playtex girdle and baby powder.

"Put this baby powder all over the top of your legs and on your stomach. Then wiggle into the girdle until you get it up," she said. I wore it day and night, taking it off only for a shower, squirming into it every time, pulling it up tug by tug. Mama said it would make me sweat off my excess weight, which it gradually did. And I was still wearing those two hot muslin dresses.

The emotional pain of giving up my child had come to me. It entered my body through my heart and never left me. During the day, I walked around with a plastic tumbler filled with Coca-Cola and whiskey. Looking at every baby I saw, I thought each one could be mine. Many nights, waking from a deep sleep, I would find myself on my hands and knees, looking under my bed for my son. *Where is my baby? Where is my baby?* I would ask myself. I had to find him.

Going through the Yellow Pages of a phone book, I found an attorney named Russell Blimsby. I made an appointment and went to see him. He was located in a nice office building in downtown Orlando. Sitting across from him at his big wooden desk, I looked around at the bookshelves that covered the walls of his office. He was a middle-aged man who had an air of authority and was the first lawyer I had ever talked to.

"Where do you live?" and "What does your father do?" were among his first questions. He knew from my answers that I had no family to protect me. "Yes, it can be done. You can get your baby back but it will cost a lot of money," he informed me.

He gave me hope. He added that he had a partner, another attorney, whom I must meet. Returning the next day, I met his partner, who said, "There is a way, but it will mean having sex with men for money to pay the legal bills."

This lawyer was nicely dressed in a suit and tie. He asked me to sign paperwork that he said would start the court process of finding my son. I was desperate. The pain in my heart about my baby overtook all reason. I signed the papers. When he told me to go to a local hotel and meet a man named Walter, I agreed.

This was an initiation rite of passage into prostitution, probably to make sure I would comply. Walter was a tall Black man. He met me at the hotel, then took me to his house. There he fucked me on the floor in front of his couch. The bare floor was hard. Turning my head toward the window, I saw four or five Black men outside the house looking in under the drapes, watching as Walter fucked me. My only thought was to wonder where his wife was.

Future encounters took place at the Downtowner Inn Hotel on Orange Avenue. It was a four-story building with underground parking and a restaurant. The hotel rooms were nicely furnished with maid service.

Still trying to go to school, I had enrolled at Rollins Jr. College a few months earlier. So now, after attending class, I would take the bus to the hotel, my schoolbooks with me.

After seeing Walter, who gave me the key, I went to the room and waited. Soon a man would knock on the door, come in, and we would exchange a few words.

"Hello," might be his first word to me.

"Hello," I would answer.

"Where can I put my clothes?" most would ask.

"On the extra bed there," I'd answer.

Many men would take off only their pants, leaving their shirt and socks on, but all would go to the sink where they unzipped their pants and pulled their dick out. Some washed it, but many would just dangle it, splashing water on it.

Sex, missionary-style, and then to the sink, this time using soap to really wash their dick, including the rim. Then they would leave. There were two or three men a night.

Walter came by at the end of the evening and gave me some money, very little. I thought most of the money was going to the lawyer to get my baby back for me.

One night Walter and I were walking on the outside corridor of the third or fourth story of the hotel and suddenly there was a loud splat, a crack, like a ripe watermelon, popping on the cement below. Walter looked over, then quickly pulled me back so that I would not see what had happened. He hurried me out of there. Sirens came. The next evening Walter told me a woman had jumped from the roof, hit the cement, and cracked her head open, committing suicide.

One man forever changed me, reached into the depths of me, and took something that could never be replaced. All the men tried to make me cum. But one man had me stand up on the bed, naked, legs spread apart while he put his head between my legs and licked my clit. I came. And I hated him for that. He took something that was innately mine.

Prostitution rips out the soul. It eats into the guts, the essence of who we are, and feeds on the hatred and disgust already there. The pain is so bad you just want to kill it and hurt yourself to get the pain out. Soon you feel nothing, just dead. Nothing. Your body walks around in a shell. From there the rest is easy. The use of drugs, smack, coke, anything, is to feel. Just so you can try to get feelings back into your soul again. I was headed into the depths of hell.

∷

Mama knew something. Returning late one night, I was sitting on the edge of my bed, the single bed with the aqua and white scratchy chenille bedspread from my high school days, when she hollered from her room, "You are doing something, I know you are doing something." I had been giving her money, too much money.

My activities lasted a few months. Then I got busted.

I should have known it was a setup because for the first time there was another couple in the room. The prostitute was Black, her john was white.

The room had double beds. They were in the first bed so my john and I got naked, then into the second bed. Soon we heard banging at the door. The door was kicked hard, then slammed open.

Four burly men burst into the room with cameras. The flashbulbs from their 1960s cameras popped and popped, giving off a blue color with each flash as we pulled the covers up around us. "You're under arrest for prostitution," one of them yelled.

"Get up, get dressed, we're going to the station," the policemen barked.

Each of us scrambled for our clothes.

Many years would pass before I could have my picture taken. Even today when I face a camera, there is a flash of memory, making my face go tight.

Arriving at the police station, I put my schoolbooks from Rollins College on the chair beside me, which caught the attention of the arresting officers.

The policeman asked me standard questions.

"Your name?"

"Diana Essig," I said quietly.

"How old are you?" he continued.

"Nineteen."

I was booked, then released late at night on my own recognizance. I picked up my books and took the bus home.

The next day, as I rode in the backseat of a friend's car, news of my arrest came on the radio.

The announcer gave details of the raid, including my name. I felt my friend's body go rigid. Burning shame filled my entire being as the car continued to my house. There were no good-byes as I got out of the car.

The news made the evening edition of the *Orlando Evening Star* newspaper:

"A Rollins College Co-Ed And A Barmaid Caught in Vice-Squad Raid."

My misery was complete.

Entering the house, I saw Mama was seated again in the round, pink chair. I did not say anything. What could I say? Any avenue of communication between us had long been broken.

I don't know what I felt, I don't remember. I have blocked out the depth and embarrassment of that pain. For the second time in my life, I could not go to sleep that night.

Mama told me later what had happened when she heard the news of my arrest.

"I was having dinner with a rancher, a nice, wealthy man who was a husband prospect for me," Mama said. "When I told him my news, he put his napkin over his uneaten food and left." She could not hold her head up.

I have no recall of the court outcome, or even going to court. Later, I found an article about my arrest that detailed the charges and said I had a fine of four hundred dollars. Mama must have paid it.

Mama couldn't take the pain and embarrassment she felt in the neighborhood and around town. She sold the house and moved away from Orlando, leaving my brother Don without a home when he was barely eighteen and just graduated from high school. Now he had to be on his own in the world.

News of my arrest had traveled to Robert, who was living in Denver. I heard he stood up for my honor, but it was Don who took the brunt of it. Still in town, he got into many fistfights, defending me.

It would be over two years before I saw Mama again and many years before we celebrated a birthday or Christmas together.

"Come stay with me and my mother in Miami Beach," said Rene, a casual friend I had met at our flophouse apartment in Orlando, after I called her.

Rene's mother drank, had a luxurious condo, and did not keep good track of her daughter. It didn't matter that I moved in; nobody noticed.

I changed my name to Elizabeth Diane Parkyns, thinking I could start a new life, but nothing changed. I drank, went to parties, and stayed out late.

Carol Young and I had stayed in touch. During one of our phone conversations, I knew she had read the newspaper article about me when she said, "If you're going to do it, come with me and do it right." Still living at Rene's mother's condo, I spent the next few months finding out what it was like to be an expensive call girl.

The Young sisters, Carol and Mary, lived in a house in Miami and made it easy for me to visit with them.

"We get five hundred dollars for an overnight, but since you are new, you will be paid two hundred fifty dollars," Carol told me.

An overnight consisted of looking pretty, lounging around before dinner and talking with men who were rich and powerful. Then dinner at a fine restaurant, returning to the house for sex. Call girls were supposed to be pretty, but I never felt pretty. I still wasn't feeling much of anything.

Carol taught me how to walk. When going through a bar, she told me to put one high-heeled foot in front of the other, keep my back straight, and hold my head high. Hold it high because I was somebody.

"And never let me catch you sitting on a bar stool after you are thirty," she added.

Mary and Carol were 5'10" tall with beautiful figures. They looked gorgeous when they were all dressed up for the evening.

"Let us dress you for our dinner tonight," Carol said. I agreed and they loaned me a black silk dress and a string of pearls. They did my makeup and put my long dark hair on top of my head.

Our evenings were planned with their clients. One night a wealthy real estate developer named Jim Walter hosted the party. During dinner in an expensive restaurant, Jim gave me his solid gold Dunhill lighter, passing it down the table to me. It was supposed to be an impressive move, but I felt awkward, and knew I did not belong there. After a few months with the Young sisters, I decided that I couldn't do this anymore. Deep within me, I knew it was wrong.

I called my friend Rose Marie Stroud, who had been my childhood neighbor in Azalea Park. She was living in Palatka, Florida, working as an insurance adjuster.

"Can I come and live with you, Rose Marie?" I asked. "I'll get a job and pay half the rent." When she said yes, I packed my clothes into my car and made the drive to Palatka. I soon found work as a waitress in an upscale restaurant.

One night I was so hungry that I took a big bite of someone's leftover steak that had been returned to the kitchen. I could not swallow it. With the piece of meat stuck in my throat, choking violently, I ran into the dining area waving my arms in the air. A man came running to me and pounded hard on my back. The piece of steak flew from my throat.

"Thank you," I said gratefully.

"My name is John Marsell," he answered. "Please give me your telephone number, young lady, so I can call you and make sure you are okay."

I gave him my number. When he called, he invited me out to dinner. We started going out often.

John was eight years older than me, tall, lean, and oozed Southern charm. This came partly from his good looks and partly because he had a lot of money. Following in his father's footsteps as one of the largest fern growers in America, he drove a white pickup truck and wore a cowboy hat and expensive boots.

Not talking much, he often said, "I reckon," which covered a lot of his thoughts. He called me "Hot Shot" as a term of endearment.

He took me on his boat to fish for grouper, then flew me around in his double-engine Cessna plane. We became lovers.

"I'm married, my wife does not understand me, and I have colon cancer," he told me.

John had to travel to New Orleans for frequent treatments of his illness. He flew his plane there and back. I enjoyed these trips with him. Once, one of the engines died and the plane dropped suddenly, making a loud whooshing sound. John looked at me and I looked at him. I guess he thought he was going to die from colon cancer anyway, and I wasn't afraid of anything. The second engine sputtered, turned over, and we kept going. We landed safely.

"I'm looking for land to start a fern farm outside of the States," John said in one of our conversations.

::
::

We began visiting Costa Rica. San Jose, the capital and Costa Rica's largest city, was our base as we traveled the country, looking for land.

Living there was primitive and peaceful. At dawn, roosters crowed, signaling it was time to get up. A woman brought a bucket of water and soap to wash my hair, and the day began. John and I usually went into town to have breakfast and when we met people, he introduced me as his wife.

John's new Range Rover made travel in the countryside over crude dirt roads comfortable, but looking at people living in shacks and cardboard, them looking back at me, I felt the huge divide. The people in town seemed happier, and the food was plentiful and delicious.

One night, John and I walked to dinner at a local restaurant.

"We have landed on the moon," John said, pointing to posters on walls of buildings that announced the moon landing in America. It was 1969 and I was twenty-two. I felt like I was on another planet hearing this news while in a foreign country.

∴

I knew he was married, but sex predominated. When he told me, "I have rented an apartment for us in Altamonte Springs," a small town north of Orlando, I thought I'd hit the jackpot, and fell hard in love with him.

Once I was settled, I called my brother Don to let him know where I was. He had kept in touch with Mama who lived nearby, and he gave her my telephone number. When she called, we were able to reconnect after our long absence.

"I met a retired army officer named Dick Becker and we're going to get married," she told me. "Please come over and meet him." After my first few visits, I told her about John.

"Why don't you and John come and visit?" Mama asked.

And so John and I visited Mama together.

"Please call me E.J.," she said to John. Then she looked at me, saying, "And honey, you can too." It felt right.

John and E.J. got along well. At her wedding, John said to her, "E.J., you don't have to do this." But she could not see any other way to support herself.

My life with John felt wonderful and stable. I drove his 1969 orange Pontiac GTO and charged an expensive wardrobe to his credit card. His generosity made it possible for me to go back to school. I enrolled at Lake-Sumter Junior College in nearby Leesburg, eventually getting an Associate of Arts Degree, cheating on every exam.

I reconnected with the Young sisters, who had given up being call girls. Carol and her new boyfriend Steve rented a house in Altamonte Springs near John and me. Mary Young married and also moved close by. Carol, Mary, and I spent afternoons at the pool, continuing our friendship.

Cooking dinner for John at night, I felt domesticated, but we were playing house. John started acting strangely, not coming home until late, losing interest in me. Sitting in a chaise lounge chair one afternoon, John looked at me and said, "You look as old as my wife." This was a telling statement.

"Let's find out what he's doing," Carol said after John had supposedly made a trip to Costa Rica alone. We went through his luggage and found, in addition to his passport, another passport with the name and photo of a young woman.

I confronted John, and we had a terrible fight.

The night John left me I made a fool of myself, as only an insecure woman can do.

"Please don't leave me. Oh please don't leave me, John."

I lay on the floor, crying ferociously, losing all my pride. While I hung onto his boots, John dragged me to the doorway.

Hanging onto his boots, I would not let him walk out the door. I grabbed one of his legs, then the other, as he tried to pry me loose. Finally, when I was exhausted, he made his getaway.

I called E.J. and continued crying long and hard. Sitting on the floor and putting my head on the bed, my tears soaked the mattress completely through to the floor. I could not stop crying. Then I called Carol.

"Come and stay in our extra bedroom," Carol said. I packed up my clothes and carried them over to their place.

• •
• •

I found a job at Maryland Fried Chicken, on Lee Road and Edgewater Drive. I swept the floors, cleaned the tables, and worked the cash register. If a person ordered three dinners, I would ring up two, keeping mental track of how many dinners I did not ring up. Then, at the end of the night, I would pocket the money for the dinners I did not ring up.

Stealing, drinking, and cheating were part of my self-destructive behavior. After being raped, going through the loss of my child, and becoming a prostitute, I was mad at the world.

In the back room, I took chicken from big baskets and then put it into a large open pan of hot grease. While I worked, the owner sat in his chair in this dark room and leered at me.

Returning to the house each night, I went straight to my bedroom and took off all my clothes. The smell of chicken grease was in my white uniform and even in my underwear. I put everything directly in the washer and dryer, then shampooed my hair to get rid of the fried chicken smell. That odor never did come out of my clothes or my hair completely.

Life at Carol and Steve's was fairly routine, but one morning I went to the kitchen, opened the refrigerator door and saw a baby doe, skinned, hung upside down by its hooves and still dripping its blood onto the floor of the refrigerator. I shut the door.

E.J. came to see me one afternoon at work. She saw me taking orders and sweeping the floor.

"Can't you find any other way?" she asked in a plaintive voice. This would not be the last time she asked that question.

∷

I became pregnant again, with no idea who the father was. There was little sex education at that time. Women used the "rhythm method," which meant counting the days from period to period and not having sex in the middle. This did not work for me because my periods were always a different length. I didn't know about other types of birth control.

"What in the world are you doing?" Carol asked me when she saw me use boiling water to sterilize a coat hanger that I had straightened out.

Carol realized that I was up to something when I asked her if she knew details on how to perform an abortion. I spent a lot of time sitting on the toilet trying to end my pregnancy. One day, I was in the bathroom with a coat hanger up my vagina. A big man looked in the window, startling me. He was only two feet away. This peeping Tom scared me and I quit trying to give myself an abortion. But I was desperate. I couldn't feel anything but pain about my body and being pregnant, not knowing who I could stay with or where I could go. I felt I had no choice.

Carol took over, knowing something had to be done. She took me to a local bar in the neighborhood that catered to men. After a few drinks, Carol introduced me to some of her friends.

"This girl is pregnant and needs an abortion. Because they are illegal here, she needs a thousand dollars to go to New York

City to get it done." The money was raised and I flew to New York, a name and address in my pocket. I had the abortion, left, and fainted on the sidewalk. Someone helped me to the airport and I got back to Steve and Carol's house.

∷

Once back in Florida, I got into a scheme with Carol and Steve. He was using fake cashier's checks to make money. These checks were routinely accepted and could be cashed at stores for a purchase with the change given back in cash.

"Come with Carol and me when we cash the checks so you can learn how to do it," he coaxed.

Carol and I went into a store while Steve waited in the car. The clerk asked me if the check was good. I looked him square in eye.

"Yes, the check is good," I lied.

"If this isn't good, it will hurt me and my family."

He cashed the check. I can still feel his eyes on me.

After a few months, Carol called me at work.

"You have to get out of town fast. The cops are on to us."

Carol knew people. She and I made up the name Julie Lynn Summers and in a few days I met a man downtown who gave me a driver's license and social security card with my new identity.

I packed my belongings, minus my yearbook and all things that reminded me of Diana Essig. Then I got a map showing the way to California, a place that held my dreams.

∷

When I was a young child, E.J. had told me stories of when she and Daddy lived there during Daddy's showbiz days. Drawing on the allure of the movies, she told me they lived in a white Spanish-style house. When she told me of their nights at the Coconut Grove, a beautiful nightclub, with famous bands and glamorous people, I knew I wanted to live there someday. I knew that Los Angeles was where I would make my fortune.

Legitimately.

::

With a small U-Haul behind my old car, I began the drive from Orlando to Los Angeles. The car had a musty-smelling heater. When I turned it on, roaches would come out and crawl up my sleeves. So I kept the heater off most of the time.

I worked out a signal with the phone so E.J. would know I was safe every night. When I stopped for the night I would call her, let the phone ring twice, and then hang up. Then I would call back with a collect call from a made-up name. She would answer, ask where the call was coming from, then decline it. This way she knew where I was.

The drive was uneventful, although I did get up one day and traveled the entire day the wrong way, and had a car repair in New Mexico that cost way too much money. Aside from that, it was a beautiful drive across America.

It was 1971, I was twenty-four years old, and starting my new life.

Mama in Pink Round Chair

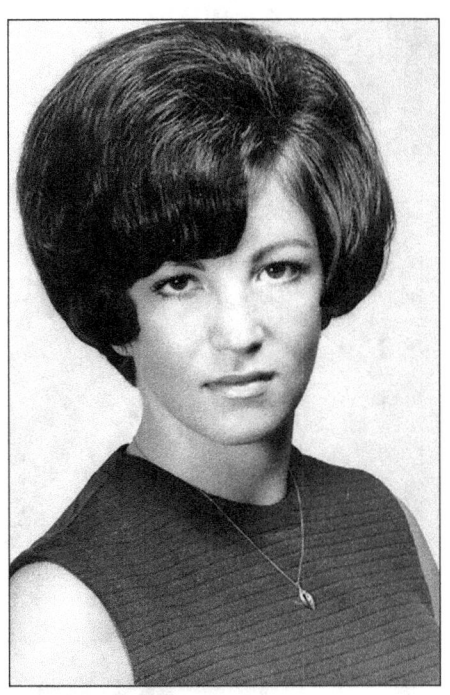
College Days

John Marsell and Orange GTO

John and I in Costa Rica

Carol and I Dressed for Dinner

ORLANDO EVENING STAR

Page 3—A
Monday, Sept. 18, 1967

Trial Set For Coed, Barmaid

A former Rollins College coed and a barmaid at the Everready Club, Parramore and Carter Sts. will be tried at noon Sept. 29 in municipal court on charges of prostitution.

The two women, Miss Diana Rae Essig, 20, 6008 Dahlia Drive, a former Rollins student and substitute teacher, and Miss Mona Davis, 22, Lincoln Arms Apts., on W. Church St., were charged with prostitution following a vice raid Wednesday at the Downtowner Motor Inn, 264 S. Orange Ave.

Walter Lee Young, 27, 2134 Jacobs St., Apt. C., a bellhop at the Downtowner, will also be tried Sept. 29 by Municipal Judge Tom Kirkland on charges of procuring for prostitution.

Barmaid, Coed Held In Vice Raid

A Rollins College student was one of two women arrested on charges of prostitution in a Wednesday night vice raid at the Downtowner Motor Inn at 264 S. Orange Ave., police said Thursday.

This was the second raid for this motel in a month, police said.

ACCORDING to the Orlando Police Dept., Miss Diana Rae Essig, 20, of 6008 Dahlia Drive, Orlando, identified herself as a student at Rollins College and a substitute teacher.

She and Miss Mona Davis, 22, a Negro, of the Lincoln Arms Apts. on West Church Street, who gave her occupation as a barmaid at the Everready Club on Parramore and Carter Sts., were charged with prostitution.

Walter Lee Young, 27, a Negro bellhop at the Downtowner, 2134 S. Jacobs St., Apt. C., was charged with procuring.

Bond was set at $500 each, a spokesman for the Orlando Police Department Vice Control Division said.

Chapter Four

LOS ANGELES

Seeing Los Angeles for the first time, driving into the city from the 118 freeway, was magic. Coming to make my fortune, I felt the possibilities of the city and loved it at first sight.

I drove south and randomly picked a freeway exit. When I saw a sign that said "First month's rent free" on an apartment building, I stopped, filled out an application, and got an apartment. It was in the city of Garden Grove.

I unpacked and returned the U-Haul.

The next night, I put on a white jumpsuit and white boots and drove to the nearest local bar. Standing inside the front door, I looked around.

"Come sit beside me. I'll buy you a drink," a man called out. "My name is Pete," he told me.

"Julie," I said as I sat on a bar stool beside him.

Pete told me about a start-up West Coast operation for a steamship company called United States Lines. Sipping on his drink, he explained that containers the size of a large truck were loaded onto ships that carried goods into and out of the country. I let him know I was looking for a job.

"Can you type?" he asked me.

"Yes," I replied.

I went to his office the next day and filled out the necessary paperwork for my new job. My workspace was in a trailer parked near the ocean in Long Beach. "Go to the third one on the right," were my instructions the day I started work. After I entered, I walked past other people who sat typing and talking loudly on their phones to my desk located at the back.

My job, outbound documentation, meant receiving paperwork from companies that shipped their goods overseas, then typing manifests for each container to be loaded onto the ships for overseas.

"Hi, my name is Vince, and I'm the manager," a good-looking Italian man said. Vince smoked cigarettes, drank coffee, and spoke with great authority. His desk was directly in front of mine, which made it easy for us to get to know each other.

"Stay for a while and help me get this out," Vince told me. He began talking about the shipping business. After the others went home, Vince and I worked late into the night. He talked and talked, explaining how exporters got their goods from the United States to the final destination overseas.

"Let's go get a drink," Vince said after another late evening. That led to, "Let me see where you live."

We began an affair. Vince and I continued to work late into the night. "You can work really long hours," I said to him one night. "How do you do that?"

He held out his hand where he had several capsules.

"Here, these will give you extra energy," Vince said as he handed me some pills. "They're called bennies because they're made of benzedrine. Don't take too many and never take one late at night."

My addiction to speed began.

∷

On E.J.'s next call to me, her voice sounded strange.

"Honey, the police are trying to find you. Did you cash some checks that weren't yours?"

My past in Florida had caught up with me.

The Orlando Police Department had a warrant for my arrest. They'd questioned E.J. and her husband many times to find out where I was. E.J. refused to tell them. She hid my letters from her husband, which caused trouble in their marriage. When the police told E.J. they had a summons from the grand jury requesting her appearance to tell them my whereabouts, she knew she would have to comply, and gave them my address.

One day I answered my phone at work.

"Is this Julie Summers, also known as Diana Essig?" a man's voice asked. "We have been contacted by the detectives in Orlando about checks you have written." It was a detective from the Los Angeles Police Department. He gave me the option of meeting him at work, or at my apartment. I agreed to meet him at home.

Sitting on my brown patterned couch in the living room, the detective asked if I had cashed phony cashier's checks. Knowing I was caught, I looked him in the eye, and replied, "Yes, sir, I did."

Everything was quiet for a few weeks. Then he called again and said, "You are one lucky girl. Your friend Carol Young died in childbirth. She was a witness, so we have no case now."

I didn't feel lucky hearing that my friend had died. But I was relieved that they wouldn't arrest me.

Vince and I began talking marriage.

When I told E.J. the news on one of our phone calls, I said, "Oh, he is so handsome, but he likes to drink a lot. He laughed and called me stupid when I couldn't read a map, but I love him."

E.J. called me a few days later. "I'm flying to Los Angeles to visit you."

This took me by surprise. She stayed a week, then left. Soon after her departure, Vince and I broke up. I have no idea what E.J. said to him, but we were done. Her disapproval of our relationship made me end it. Feeling uncomfortable with Vince in such close proximity to me at work, I made an appointment for a job interview with the manager at a customhouse brokerage firm.

A customhouse brokerage firm is a company with a broker who is licensed by the Treasury Department. Under the responsibility of the broker, the work of the firm is to determine all legal aspects, along with the tariff rate, on goods coming into the country. And then to get the shipment, usually brought in by container, to its final destination by way of rail, truck, or air.

"It's okay that you are a few minutes late," Moses Shamash said when I arrived. As the manager and broker of James J. Boyle Co., he interviewed and then hired me.

Moses was a Sephardic Jew from Rangoon, Burma, now Myanmar. He had survived the Japanese occupation during World War II, and migrated to the United States. He had a pleasant appearance, with curly hair, kind yet piercing eyes, and a ready smile. My job was to handle inbound documentation, which meant preparing waybills to move cargo off the dock. Having worked outbound documentation at United States lines, this furthered my knowledge of the shipping business.

Going to work every day became my life, and I worked long unpaid hours after quitting time. Moses saw my dedication, and my first promotion came within a few months. I began to understand the business, which I found fascinating.

Not having Vince to supply me with bennies, I had to look for another source. I found a doctor in the phone book who prescribed diet pills. My tolerance to the drug increased, as did my need for more pills. I worked late, took more diet pills, and began a vicious cycle of work, little sleep, and more pills.

Moses began taking more interest in me. We didn't have a romantic relationship, but he looked after me.

"I don't want you to make the long drive from Garden Grove to downtown Los Angeles," he told me one day. Then he found an apartment for me on S. Doheny Drive in Beverly Hills. I called E.J., who was divorced after being married a few short years. Then I called Gram, Don, and Robert, asking them all to visit.

One by one they came. Moses paid the bills in return for my hard work at the office. His generosity let me show my family a good time in Palm Springs, Las Vegas, and of course, the Sunset Strip. I was so happy to be reunited with my family.

Moses took me and another woman, Anna, under his wing. He wanted us to get our broker's licenses. Anna's desk sat directly next to mine and after my last promotion, she and I held the top two positions in the office of about fifteen people. Moses tutored us privately and individually to help us understand the complexities of the customhouse brokerage business. Because there were no classes at that time to teach the business, a person had to read large and extensive books published by the Department of the Treasury before taking an exam for a license.

"I will be over tonight at seven o'clock," Moses said to me many nights after work. He came to my apartment with books under his arm. I listened as he read, in his soft and lilting voice, the laws and regulations of importing. He would listen patiently as I explained them back to him. We worked like this for two years. I began to understand that the reason for his tutoring Anna and me was that he wanted to start his own business.

∴∴

E.J. was still living in Florida. She worked as a telephone solicitor, a job with constant rejection. She sounded very depressed when we spoke on the phone, and my heart ached for her.

"Honey, I am eating a lot of hard-boiled eggs. I'm even putting water in my mascara to make it last longer," E.J. told me.

I told Moses about E.J.'s situation, hoping he would offer to help. He did. "E.J., Moses said he would help you find a job if you move out to L.A."

I persuaded her to move. We chose an apartment for her nearby on Kings Road in West Hollywood. Moses found her a job as a clerk at a discount department store, which meant standing on her feet all day. It paid most of her bills so I supplemented the remainder.

"Ask E.J. when she can go to dinner and we will go to Chasen's," Moses said.

Chasen's, a popular restaurant in Beverly Hills made famous by Elizabeth Taylor and her love for their chili, began our fine dining experiences. Moses always took E.J. with us. Most of Chasen's patrons were famous movie stars or important people who worked in entertainment. When E.J. walked in, the clientele gave her the once over to see if she were one of them. When they saw that she wasn't famous, people returned their attention to their meals.

Over at Scandia, one of the fanciest restaurants on the famed Sunset Strip, waiters lined up against the wall. They wore uniforms and white gloves as they discreetly waited to see if their service was needed. I ordered chicken wrapped in a basket that looked like twigs.

"You can eat the twigs," Moses said.

Edible twigs were new to me. Through this luxury, I saw the beginning of another world.

E.J. and I learned how to spend time together. We began spending holidays eating at expensive restaurants, just the two of us, and gradually our communication grew stronger.

∵∴

After two tries, I passed the customhouse brokerage exam. Starting my own business on October 15, 1975, I named it J.D. Summers Co. I was 28 years old.

When I told Moses of my plans, he talked long and hard, asking me to stay with him.

"Why don't you wait for a year or two? We can go into business together," Moses suggested.

But I would not listen to him. Two years seemed like an eternity to me. This was something I had to do now. So I turned his offer down.

The antique trade intrigued me. My first account was one I took with me from James J. Boyle. The Antique Guild, located at the former Helms Bakery site on Venice Boulevard, brought in four containers of antiques a day. Soon I had other accounts, meeting my first year's projection of net $35,000. I may have been the first woman customs broker in Los Angeles. But I was completely hooked on the amphetamine in diet pills. Even though my business was successful, I had no sense of myself.

E.J. was my first employee. "I found the perfect office," she said to me one day. "It's at 311 Ocean Boulevard in Long Beach, in a building located over The Pike. We can have lunch and go for a walk on the boardwalk of the amusement park."

The antique business was just starting in Los Angeles and my business took off. Word of mouth told me who was importing, and I recruited new clients. Our business agreements were done verbally, as was a lot of business at that time.

E.J. used the voluminous tariff books to classify the documents, determining the duty. She was good at her job and her self-esteem improved tremendously. Soon, I had two additional employees and was clearing close to $100,000 a year. Thinking I had a lot more money than I did, I used the cash flow from clients' money, meant for duty and other transportation expenses, for my drug habit, never realizing it would catch up with me.

∷

I moved to a one-bedroom apartment in a complex on Sunset Boulevard in Brentwood. E.J. moved to Costa Mesa in Orange County. Our relationship was better. Now that we worked together we had more things to talk about. "I'll be there in an hour," was my reply to E.J.'s invitation to our Sunday dinners. Driving my new, blue BMW straight down the 405 freeway made it easy.

E.J. and I loved going to hit musicals and plays around town. One night we caught Joan Rivers' act in a small nightclub in Beverly Hills. But when I took E.J. to Las Vegas, the city had an unexpected blackout, furthering my belief that E.J.'s luck in life was not the best.

E.J., a good artist herself, wanted to go to the annual summer Festival of the Arts art fair in Laguna Beach, next to Pageant of the Masters. We spent a Sunday buying paintings, mine mostly of seascapes. E.J. loved clowns.

Looking at her new purchase of a clown painting she said, "I am like the clown who makes everyone laugh. Then I go home, take off my makeup, and the tears slide down my cheeks."

The way she said it made me laugh. I loved the way she told a story about herself, not realizing her humor was self-deprecating.

Sitting in her apartment one Sunday, I looked at her and said, "Let's go to Disneyland." We spent the day like children in a big playground, both of us having a wonderful time. These were important days for me. I caught a glimpse into who my mother was as a person and we shared a different relationship. I began to realize my mother loved me very much.

∷

Her love for me couldn't stop my downward spiral. I was hell-bent on destruction. I couldn't control how many diet pills I was taking, smoked three packs of cigarettes a day, and got very little sleep. I could not tell one day from the next. Waking up from a very deep sleep and not knowing what day it was, I dialed zero on the telephone.

"What time is it, operator? And what day is it, please?"

I was losing touch with reality.

When I was twenty-four hours late for an appointment with a client, I didn't take it as a warning sign. But E.J. was alarmed. She knew I had asked my employees to go to the doctor to get more diet pills for me.

E.J. tried to stop them, knowing the pills were killing me. Later, when I asked her why she didn't help me, put me into an institution, or anywhere, to dry out, she said, "Because I wanted to be your friend."

Because of the pills, I walked around the office building late into the night. I knew all the janitors who worked the night shift. Many nights I didn't make it home.

I was at the office the evening E.J. called, desperation in her voice. Sobbing hysterically, she said, "My Karmen has been stolen!" Karmen was the nickname for her car, a red Karmann Ghia that she loved very much. I left the office and drove for hours, aimlessly, on the freeways of Los Angeles, trying to find her car, not realizing it was futile. Returning to the office in the early morning hours, I took more pills, trying to function through the day.

∷

My business lasted four years. I sold it in 1979, or rather, I practically gave it away. The sale was done verbally. Because of my drug addiction, I did not keep track of any monies due or owed to me by the new buyer. It was a mess. I kept trying to get up in the morning and go to the office but I could not make it. Finally, I just quit going.

But I still had my checkbook and extra checks.

Moses Shamash

Moses, E.J. and Me

E.J. at Work

E.J. and I Having Fun

E.J. and I, My 30th Birthday

Visiting on Doheny Drive. Gram, Don, E.J., Me and Friend

Chapter Five

METH ADDICTION AND THE HELLS ANGELS

Cruising the streets of Brentwood late one night I met a drug dealer who said his name was David Diamond. He pulled up beside me in his new black Porsche, saying, "Do you want to go for a cup of coffee?"

About five years younger than me, with thick curly black hair, David was quite good-looking in a slick and oily way.

We connected.

David began staying with me in my apartment on Goshen Avenue in Brentwood, furnished with beautiful paintings and furniture from my clients. Disappearing for a few days, he always returned.

David introduced me to cocaine. He had a connection who gave him bags of coke to hold. These five-gallon bags sat around the apartment, two or three at a time. The coke was sparkly, white or yellow in color, depending on the shipment that had come in.

I did not realize he was a big dealer until he told me the bags were pure and uncut. He told me that when the bags were given to his connection, they were put into large plastic tubs and "washed," using an additive like baking powder or speed to make street coke.

David's dealer came to see him and to meet me, probably to check things out. We sat at the dining room table and did lines of coke. David's dealer also took a good look around at my possessions.

Living with a drug dealer had a disastrous effect on my life. David gave me small bags of his street coke, the same ones he sold to smaller dealers. Coked up badly, I could not stop picking at an imaginary bump on the bridge of my nose. This went on for many days. Each time David returned to the apartment, he found me sitting in the exact same place.

"You're scaring me. You've been picking at the same spot on your nose for days," he finally said.

Using a mirror, I dug deeper and deeper until I picked through the cartilage to a membrane until it popped, sending searing acid-like pain up and down my nose. It tore the skin on my nose apart, and left a deep ridge of a scar that will be with me for the rest of my life.

David soon realized I liked methamphetamine, meth. It was easy for him to get, and made him feel safe with his coke around me.

I liked meth because I felt strong and powerful, like I could do anything I wanted to. I felt like I was in another world, and wanted to stay there.

And the sex, constant sex, truly was out of this world.

I looked at the streetlights and the stars as if I had never seen them before. I felt young, and I loved feeling young, knowing that someday I would be old, very old.

Tweaked out, I drove the streets. When I saw a Burger King, I went to the trash, broke the big black trash bags open and looked for the cards that games were played on, promising cash. Of course, these cards were already scratched, used, but I thought somehow I would find a winning card.

Daybreak, and the sun rose on me in the Burger King parking lot, the trash spread around me. Having my bindles, small packages, of meth on me, and snorting constantly, I left, driving aimlessly before returning home.

∷

These drug days are one big blur. I had all the toxic side effects of doing speed and coke. I was paranoid. When I drove in my car, I was sure the man in the car behind me—it was always a man—had a gun, was aiming it, waiting to shoot me.

Meth will make a person steal anything, just to steal. I stole things for no reason, even clothes I could not wear, out of the dryer in the laundry room in my building. My behavior was desperate and unhinged. Thinking someone was looking in my windows, I used scissors to cut holes in the bottom of my drapes and spent nights on the floor looking out of those holes.

Vaguely realizing I had no money coming in and that I was going broke, I had my first nervous breakdown. I walked to my BMW, which was parked in the building's underground parking garage, and sat in the car. Sitting there, I watched people get out of the elevator, go to their cars, and leave for work. They returned at night, parked their cars, got into the elevator, and went home to their apartments.

I just sat there day and night and watched, in my car the entire time, getting out to pee on the garage floor close to my car. Otherwise, I did not move. It felt as if I was paralyzed. Many days and nights passed as I sat in my car, trying to go somewhere but never going anywhere.

Eventually I did make it back to my apartment where I had an occasional TV dinner, and crazy sleep. Nothing made sense, and worse, it did not matter that nothing made sense.

∷

It wasn't hard for me to feel the combination lock code on David's briefcase and click it open. There were stacks of bills in large denominations with a rubber band around each one. I slipped out a few bills from various stacks and then shut the briefcase, twirling the combination lock shut. I started doing this more and more often. When David discovered what I was doing, he went ballistic.

"You did this to me? While we were sleeping together?" he screamed at me. Grabbing his briefcase, he stormed out of my apartment.

It was an unforgivable act, especially in the drug world. I was afraid of what David and his dealer might do to me. Luckily, the only thing they did was hire a moving van to come to my apartment on a day he knew I would be gone. They moved everything out, everything but the carpet and the drapes. When I got home and saw my bare apartment, I was heartsick at losing every possession I had. And afraid of what might be next.

In a panic, I got a room to hide in at a nearby Holiday Inn. I called E.J. to tell her that I had left my apartment.

"I got a call from someone at the FBI," she said calmly. Stunned, I asked her what they said.

"They want to talk to us about your boyfriend."

"To both of us?" I was shocked.

"Just tell the truth, honey. The truth."

I couldn't imagine why they would want to speak with E.J. The agency must have been watching us or listening to our phone calls. Paranoia set in again. What would David do to me if he knew I was talking to the FBI?

E.J. called the agent back to make an appointment. On the day of the meeting, I was a wreck. I drove to her apartment and we sat on her beautiful forest green couch, with E.J. on my right and the agent on my left. I answered the questions simply, taking care not to say anything too revealing.

Most of the agent's questions were about the man who was supplying David with drugs. Luckily, I had only met him twice. The second time he visited my apartment was after David caught me stealing his money. He admired my antiques and even remarked how nice my china was. I guess he was taking inventory before he helped David take everything.

"I don't know anything about him," I answered honestly. I couldn't even remember what he looked like.

∴
∴

After the agent left, E.J. and I sat quietly for a while. Finally, she broke the silence.

"I'm moving back to Orlando," she told me.

After her job with me ended, she had been unable to find other work. Plus she knew the depths of my drug use. The dangerous connections I had in my life scared her. I looked around her apartment and saw that her dining room rug was a black mess from all the cigarette ashes she dropped on the floor. Her nerves had gone bad.

She had some diamond jewelry that I bought for her. I gave her a few thousand dollars that I had hidden from the stash in

David's briefcase. I was so out of control on drugs that I didn't even try to get her to stay.

My next blow was the repossession of my leased car. I loved that BMW so much, but had not made the payments on it. From my hotel window, I saw the tow truck hook it up and drive off. I was naked so I threw on my raincoat and ran after it screaming and crying, "Stop, stop, you're taking my car!" It wasn't long before I was evicted from my apartment for not paying the rent.

∴∴

When David and I were on good terms, he had given me the phone number of another drug dealer named Ric. I needed more meth, so I called him. Ric was big and had dark hair all over his body. His manners were crude, he swore a lot, and he was not educated. A thug. I didn't care. Ric supplied my meth.

"I'm going to find an apartment for you in Sherman Oaks. It's cheaper," Ric informed me. That was fine by me.

Once inside my new place, I got caught up in things like cleaning the toilet. I cleaned the bowl, inside the tank, and the hoses going to it, but I did it slowly, oh so slowly. Going to the living room to snort a line of meth, I would continue cleaning. Days and nights would pass, but nothing in the world, not eating or sleeping, became more important than snorting and cleaning that toilet bowl. The task was never finished.

Ric's only concern was getting money from me. He took me shopping to large stores where I wrote checks against my own overdrawn checking account. He sold the merchandise to get cash. I did not ask questions.

It was 1980 and I was thirty-three years old. Using constantly, I never went to bed for sleep.

"Come on, we're taking a drive," Ric told me one day. "There is someone I want you to meet."

When Ric introduced me to the Fachmans, I was a doped-up mess. The Fachmans, two brothers named Bobby and Sammy, were Hells Angels, and the Hells Angels had street control of my drug of choice, meth.

Ric first took me to meet Betty, the brothers' mother. Betty was a small, nice-looking woman, not old enough to be my mother. "Come in, come in and sit down. Would you like a glass of iced tea?" Betty graciously asked.

She lived in a house in the San Fernando Valley. The house was very open and clean, with several German Shepherd dogs. Almost as big as I was, they moved from couch to pool and back again. "I can see Spikey likes you the best, but they all like you," said Betty, clearly impressed by this fact.

The next time Ric and I went to Betty's we unloaded air conditioners and other merchandise. Betty excused herself, saying, "Take your time. You can store your things in this part of the garage." I never knew who fenced the items, or where most of the money went.

"Come over next Sunday," Betty said to me as we were leaving. "I will cook you dinner."

The next Sunday, I ate the casserole dinner and while we sat and drank iced tea, Betty read Tarot cards for me.

I looked around and saw the living room had walls of mirrors that reflected Betty's and my image. It occurred to me they might be there to alert her to any intruders. A separate room to the right was filled with Hindu images, with burning incense and an altar with a prayer rug on the floor. Further inside the house the rooms were darker. Wind chimes completed the atmosphere.

I went often to Betty's for Sunday dinner and a Tarot reading. During this time Ric took me to meet the brothers, Betty's sons. Close in age, they were several years younger than me, and lived in a nearby house.

∷

Dark, the house was always dark, and gave the feeling of constant evil living there. A small truck sat in the front yard that had long ago been eaten up by motorcycles. The peephole in the front door allowed for cautious entry.

Bear, a dog aptly named, as he was as big and black as one, checked people out as they came through the door. I'm sure he could be fierce, but there was a gentle side to him when, later, we would roll on the floor, playing together.

Dim lights in the living room showed other dogs and biker girls, girls with all their tattoos, who lounged on big pillows on the floor. Quiet around the house, they were called a house mouse because they did the bidding of their men without a sound. They wanted their meth too.

Beer cans rolled across the floors, ashtrays overflowed, and the beds were mattresses in different rooms. When I slept there for the first time, I saw a woman who had blonde hair on her head and on her pubic area. I could not stop staring.

I was not meant to overhear conversations and was tolerated because of my connection with Betty. The family talk was of drugs, drug deals, or crimes that were to take place, disguised so I would not know what was going on. They used words they thought were code, like "heist" or "job," or "pillage and plunder." I did not care. I was only there to get my meth.

••
••

"Take this to Betty for me," Bobby said as he handed me a sealed envelope. Back at Betty's I stood in the kitchen watching her make a sandwich for me. She said I had the best figure she had ever seen and asked which of her boys was the best in bed, letting me know she knew I had been to bed with both of them.

Later she showed me an article in the *Los Angeles Times* that had her picture in it, in uniform, as an animal rights activist, making sure I saw her holstered gun which was prominently displayed.

She talked about her boys, proud of the fact that they ran with the Angels.

"Is it true Sammy put an ice pick through someone's neck?" I asked her.

No reply came from her, but a look on her face showed me she knew the crimes they committed. She was happy to be their mother.

I remember Betty always walking me out of the house to my car; otherwise, I would not know that I had a car.

••
••

Frank the Fish, the brothers' father, had his own room at Bobby and Sammy's house. On a night when I was not there, he was shot through the back of the head, killed, possibly retaliation from one of the brothers' enemies. At Frank's funeral, Bobby showed me how to spot a disguised FBI agent. There were a lot of them. When we left, the noise from the Harley bikes was deafening.

∷

During my association with the Hell's Angels, I spent most of my time in my apartment in Sherman Oaks.

It is hard to describe the depth of addiction I was in. Taking a shower was not important and I seldom did. The kitchen overflowed with boxes, with just enough of an opening so that I could get to the refrigerator, although I do not remember eating.

All time ran simultaneously; there was no day or night. The days were not days, they were spaces of time that did not fit together neatly or have the measure of time. There were no days or months or even years. The absence of holidays and all family birthdays, mine included, did not bother me. It had been three years since I lost contact with my family.

∷

Many nights Bobby picked me up and we went to another person's apartment to "freebase." This meant putting coke in a spoon with water, then lighting the spoon underneath to inhale the fumes. Occasionally, using the same method, we would smoke "black tar," heroin. The high was euphoric, the sex was out of this world.

I pulled a heist. I never did get my cut or find out what was in the score, but it must have been a good score because, putting the pieces together today, I realize the brothers pushed me away from them.

They introduced me to a man name Whitey as a connection for my speed. Whitey was an albino who made my skin crawl and I had to give him a blow job along with cash for the meth. But Whitey was far more mainstream than the Angels. Once when I was with him we stopped at the office of his lawyer, Bill Churnes, Esq. I liked Bill, and we exchanged telephone numbers.

I called Suzy Sheranian, a former client who imported antiques from England. Over drinks, I told her I was writing bad checks for merchandise.

"Well, let's go to Palm Springs on a shopping spree," she said. This turned into quite a few sprees for expensive clothes for her, with me writing the checks. Then she had another idea.

"Let's go to England," Suzy said.

She was familiar with the country and had purchased many containers of antiques there. It sounded like a good idea.

We stayed with a family in Manchester. It was a cold flat in a cold city. My brain was mud. The trip was pointless, and I had no money. On a trip to London, I stood outside Harrods department store, looked up at it, but would not go in. I couldn't afford to buy anything. I had the equivalent of ten U.S. dollars in my purse.

I used my return plane ticket and flew back to the States, alone.

Chapter Six

JAIL

My plane arrived in Los Angeles, and, not realizing my name had been put on a list by U.S. Customs Service of criminals who had warrants for their arrest, I gave my passport to the clerk. He looked at it, looked at me, then called the police.

They escorted me to a small room at the airport where I was questioned by a female police officer. Then I was handcuffed and driven to Sybil Brand Institute, Los Angeles County women's jail.

Sybil Brand was built in 1963 on a hilltop near East Los Angeles. It was meant to house two thousand inmates, but almost immediately became overcrowded. It had to be the hellhole of the world. A female police officer met the squad car at the entrance and walked me up the narrow hallway to the jail. The building had cement walls and very few windows. "Step inside," the officer told me when we reached the holding tank, a room built for twenty to thirty women. Hard steel benches lined three sides of the room. Ceiling-to-floor bars that faced a corridor formed the fourth wall.

Smoking was allowed. Many of the women pulled out cigarettes, one after another, from packs they were holding. Nervously puffing, they paced up and down the floor.

Frightened women grabbed the bars screaming, "I'm innocent, I'm innocent, let me out of here," or "My babies, my babies, I have to get home to take care of them."

Most of us sat on the benches and smoked and talked, the women declaring their innocence. Our stories all had men behind them. We waited as new arrestees were brought in.

After many hours we heard a voice.

"We are letting you out now. Form a line in the corridor. Arms to your sides, no talking, eyes straight ahead," came the command.

Shuffling along, we reached a woman who sat on a stool behind a glass-windowed opening. Sliding a manila envelope under the opening, she gave the instructions. "Put your valuables in the envelope, seal it, and slide it back to me. It will be returned to you when you are released." I put everything into the envelope and slid the envelope under the cage, back to her. She wrote my name on the envelope and in a very bored voice, said, "Next."

After more time in line on our feet, we were sent to a room to have our fingerprints taken for police files. Forever identified.

∷

In another room we were able to sit on chairs for a short while. We answered questions about our backgrounds and were told to reveal our scars, to be used for identification. Mine was on my nose. In the last room, they put a wristband with my identification number on my wrist.

Then came the shower room. Ten or fifteen at a time, we were directed to a large room that had showerheads along the wall, spaced a few feet apart. This open room shower made cleaning our private parts embarrassing, and this lent itself to the constant jail smell of women. In daily life, when we are overlaid with the perfumed products from our society, we do not recognize our own body smell. Now, with plain soap for body and hair, our individual scent soon became apparent.

The female guards, always in uniform, gave commands.

"Get naked, drop your clothes at your feet. Go to the shower heads. One at a time."

The water came on. We showered quickly.

"Time's up," a guard yelled.

We walked the twenty feet back to the guards, stood a few feet in front of them, naked, while the next batch of women lined up to take their showers.

"Turn around, put your feet wide apart, bend over, grab your ankles and spread 'em," was the next command. The guards hosed us down with a hose larger than a garden hose. The water spray was hard, but it did not hurt. More guards came down the line and put a fine white powder on the top of our heads. This was a strong delousing shampoo to get out any lice from our hair. Then we headed back to the showers to shampoo our heads.

"Time's up," came from the guard again.

Another line, another room, this time for prison garb. I was given a blue dress and white thongs, along with a white cotton prison-issue blanket and a small pillow with a white plastic covering. I don't remember if we were assigned underwear; we must have worn our own.

∙ ∙
∙ ∙

I waited in line against a wall for my turn to make one collect phone call. Then I called Bill Churnes, the attorney I had met when I was with Whitey.

"Do not tell them about your drug use, or any people you know," Bill told me.

I had been sleeping with Bill. He agreed to represent me if I would turn over the pink slip to him on the old car that I bought after I lost my BMW.

After waiting in another line, two guards led us to our cells.

"Next four ladies, into your cell."

The cell had bunk beds against each wall. There was one sink and one toilet.

There is no worse sound in this world than hearing those metals bars slam behind you, not knowing when you will get out. My stomach hit bottom.

We didn't talk much. If one of us used the toilet, the other inmates looked away, like when a person gives a dog privacy to do their business. I did not get to know my bunkmates beyond asking their names.

::

Meals were the highlight of the day, took a lot of time, and were anxiously awaited.

At lunchtime the cells were unlocked automatically with a dull heavy metal sound.

Over the loudspeaker a guard's voice blared out:

"Lunch, lunch, step out of your cells, ladies."

"No talking, hands by your sides, look straight ahead," came the next command.

"Form a line, two abreast." Then we began the long walk to the cafeteria.

Looking a fellow inmate in the eye could be interpreted as a hostile act, a territorial act. I was able to look at the other women without being censored by them. I had no axes to grind, no battles to fight. But once I accidentally brushed the shoulder of the woman in front of me. Her reaction was scalding.

"Don't touch me, don't you touch me! I am County property!"

I jumped back. Lesson learned.

∷

The guards, called matrons, had a mantra. Speaking hard and deep, they walked up and down the lines, repeating often, "Ladies, no talking, hands by your sides. Look straight ahead."

Turning around in line, I accidentally looked directly at a matron, violating an unwritten rule. She picked me up by my neck, yanking me off my feet, and slammed me against the wall. Fear of knowing I had done nothing wrong but was incapable of defending myself came to me. I went limp. She let me slide to the floor. I weighed no more than one hundred pounds, was old for a jail inmate, and definitely pitiful-looking.

Many of my teeth, rotten from the meth, had fallen out. Sometimes a tooth or part of a tooth would fall out while I was walking across a room. There was no pain, no nothing. Just another smelly, rotten stump in my mouth. A lot of my hair fell out, and my paper-thin nails had deep ridges. I did not present a very aggressive or pretty picture.

∷

At the cafeteria, our eyes down, walking two abreast, we waited at the doorway. Four matrons, two on each side of the doorway, carefully scrutinized us as we entered. Filing into a single line, we took our metal trays and walked slowly in front of the counter. Other inmates dropped the food, scoop by scoop, onto our trays. The food was hot and there was enough of it.

We sat at small square tables on round-seated stools that had no back, all made of stainless steel. The stools were bolted to the ground and we had to eat with our cellmates. The room had approximately twenty-five tables.

"Time's up, ladies, time's up, ladies, back to your bunks," came from the matrons.

We stood up from the tables and formed a line. Guards scrutinized us as we walked by them on our return to our cells. By the time we got back a great deal of the day was taken up, and with three meals a day, it made time pass.

∴

"Count, head count," blared the guards at night.

We extended our wrists through the bars so a guard could come by and check the numbers we had been given on our wristbands.

"Lights out, no talking," came over the loudspeaker, repeated many times.

Another day ended.

∴

There were small windows high on the wall of some corridors, but no rays of sun ever shone into the cells. Once a week, we were allowed to walk around the perimeter of the outside yard for twenty minutes.

∴

I spent a Christmas at "Sybil's House," as the girls liked to call it. The day was lightened when Sybil Brand came to every jail cell and stepped inside. The guards watching carefully, she gave each of us a small bag that contained some makeup and pieces of chocolate.

∴∴

On Saturday afternoons, we were shuffled into a large room that had a television. About forty of us sat on the floor, watched TV, and talked with other inmates. Most of the talk was of families and children. Some women talked of their crimes, always saying they were innocent.

Little acts of kindness passed between us. One of my cellmates showed me how to fix my hair with the cardboard rolls that are inside toilet paper, so that I could try to look decent on the days I had to go to court.

"Court, Summers!" a matron yelled into my cell.

This was notice that I would have to be up early the next day for my court appearance.

In the morning, I was awakened before dawn. After waiting in the long lines, then eating breakfast, I was moved to a large cell with other women who were also going to court. We waited for the bus that would take us.

"Summers, step to the side," I was told by a big burly male guard. "You are considered a high risk, so we need to shackle you."

My recent return from a foreign country made me different from the others. I was considered a flight risk. The guards put chains around my wrists and my waist, with a long chain leading down to my ankles, which were then shackled.

The prison buses were big with tinted windows and black-and-white lettering on each side saying "County of Los Angeles Sheriff's Department." I was the last to get on the bus because I was shackled. My seat was near the front.

Looking out the window, I imagined myself as I used to be, driving the streets in my blue BMW, with places to go and things to do. I looked at the streets of LA, the city I loved. Reality began to seep in. I started to wonder how I had come to this.

Getting off the bus with the other inmates, we were taken to a large holding cell where we waited our turn to see the judge. At lunchtime, the guards handed each of us a small bag with a sandwich and an apple. I reached through the bars to get my lunch, but I couldn't eat the crust of the bread or the apple. I had lost too many teeth.

∷

I had written checks all over Los Angeles, Ventura County, and Palm Springs so I had to be arraigned at each court near where the crime was committed. I had to go to many different courts and ride the prison buses many different times. My attorney met me at every court appearance.

My bail was set at a high amount because I had written many checks in multiple counties. It was also high because I was arrested upon returning from England. I was arraigned and taken before the judge in each courtroom. The judge told me why I was arrested, which was writing checks against my own overdrawn checking account, and asked me to enter a plea. I always pled guilty.

My attorney explained to each judge about my prior earning capacity and my customhouse brokerage business. He also told the judge about the other cases. Finally, he asked for a consolidation of these cases, along with a reduced bail. This, along with my guilty pleas, probably influenced the judge.

"Granted," said the judge. He reduced the bail amount, then banged his gavel.

When my cellmates learned about my high bail amount, they wanted to know where my "corner" was. This was their joke, implying that I was a prostitute working on the street. They could not imagine a woman getting arrested for writing bad checks for large sums of money on her own bank account.

∷

Jules Salkin, one of my clients when I had my customhouse brokerage business, paid my bail. The amount he paid was ten per cent of the bail that the judge set, along with a certified promise that if I skipped, he would pay the entire amount to the court.

Jules owned a large antiques store. On the day I had an appointment with him to get his business, I had worn tight jeans, a white blouse, and nice leather boots. He asked me to dinner and gave me his account. He was single and we began our affair. Tall with a lean build, Jules had white hair and was more than thirty years older than me.

In addition to having a very successful antiques store, Jules was an attorney and a recognized architect who'd studied under Frank Lloyd Wright. He had conducted a well-known orchestra in England and was a member of Mensa, an organization for people who score at the 98th percentile or higher on an IQ test.

Jules had an impressive background, but he also had a dark side. He had defrauded the Small Business Association of almost half a million dollars. The FBI arrested him for the largest case of tax evasion at that time. He was sentenced to eighteen months in prison in Lompoc, California. I made the drive frequently to see him.

When I called him to bail me out, he was not happy, but he did it. I had little focus or sense of time, but the time served at Sybil Brand must have been two or three months.

Off My Knees

∷

I wrote the following poem about my time at Sybil Brand:

SYBIL'S HOUSE

I'm on my way to Sybil's house, to get her brand
 on me,
Sybil's house, Sybil Brand, ain't no place to be.

Waitin' here at Sybil's house, wrists cuffed behind
 my back
Within her walls, behind locked doors, stomach feels
 like lead.

Damn the hash that we must eat, shufflin' hallways
 with our feet.
Matrons from the very first, "Officah, Officah," we
 could burst.

"Ladies this" and "Ladies that," "No talking, straight
 ahead.
Gates close to form steel bars, doors clangin' in
 my head.

Time served at Sybil's house, ain't never comin' back,
Gonna quit my man, start "pickin' up," and makin'
 with that track.

I learned a lot at Sybil's house, gonna scrub her brand
 off me,

Sybil's house, Sybil Brand, ain't no place to be.

When I left the jail, the manila envelope containing valuables was returned to me. My attorney rented a small grungy apartment on Hillside Drive. I walked into the apartment, knelt in a corner, and dumped the contents of the manila envelope onto the floor. Everything came out in a jumble: pictures of E.J. and the family, cards from places I had joined (the kind one has when trying to make their way up in the world), my driver's license, and a tube of lipstick.

My shoulders hunched over as I saw how I was ruining my life. I tried to put things back into my wallet in the same order as before. Nothing fit. I crawled over to the carpet, lay down, and cried. But when I got up again, I made a call for more meth, and continued to use.

My attorney kept in touch with me. He came over early every morning to have sex. I checked in with Jules once a week, and I was still driving my old car.

I stayed in touch with E.J. by phone. I cannot imagine what I put her through, but I wasn't thinking about her, I was only thinking about meth. She always put on a brave face, and by this time there was no one left for me but her. I had thoroughly burned every bridge to every business acquaintance, every friend, and every family member.

Off My Knees

The Devil was after my soul. I walked the nearby streets looking for open garages that might have something I could steal to pay for my drugs.

I stole anything I could to buy meth. I slept on a mattress I dragged in off the street. I drank gallon jugs of a sugary fruit drink and ate Nestlé Crunch candy bars. But that apartment had a bird's eye view of the city, and, looking out the window late at night, I vowed that one day, Los Angeles would be mine.

∷

Still out on bail from Sybil Brand, I remained drug-crazed. I called Sammy Fachman and told him about a person who owed me money from when I had my business. We decided to go to their house. I was sure the house had no alarms and a lot of small valuable antiques inside.

Arriving at the house, we pried a window open. I put one foot on the floor and the alarms went off. We ran around to the front of the house right into a squad of police cars. They threw us onto the sidewalk, hard. My wrists were cuffed behind my back, then I was put into a police car.

Because the house was in Orange County, we were taken to Orange County Jail, where I was booked for burglary. By now I knew the routine, and eventually I was put into a cell with other girls.

While I was getting ready for the night, I turned my back, and two girls jumped me. The other girls in our cell sat on their cots watching while the two whirled me around to face them. Yanking on my hair, not making much noise, they tried to get my arms behind my back. Kicking, twisting, I got one good stomach punch into one of them. They backed off, deciding to leave me alone.

Sammy posted bail.

My footprint on the floor of the house I had tried to burgle identified me. The jail kept the shoes I was wearing as evidence. They could not find my clothes so they released me in my jail garb, an orange jumpsuit.

When I got back to the apartment on Hillside Drive, I put the key in the lock. The door would not open. I was locked out.

I called my attorney saying, "Bill, what happened?"

"You'll have to find another place to stay," he told me. "I don't have enough money to keep renting an apartment. Let me know where you are when you've found a place."

I called Suzy Sheranian, and we talked of our recent shopping spree in Palm Springs and trip to England. I told her I needed a place to stay. Her husband, Lincoln, had an empty condo on the river canal in Newport Beach, and Suzy told me I could move in.

After moving in, and desperate for money, I checked to make sure my upstairs neighbors weren't home. I climbed in their kitchen window, took all the cash I could find, then called Bobby Fachman, who brought me some meth.

We sat at a table in the kitchen, snorting up. Bobby looked at me and said, "Get out of the business. You make a rotten criminal."

It was the last time I saw him.

∷

There were boat slips for boats to dock, and a walkway in front of the condo. I never walked there. I kept the drapes shut but I could hear the slapping sound the boats made on the water when the winds blew, and the bells on the boats that were moored.

That Christmas, in 1982, I watched from the living room as the Newport Christmas Boat Parade went by. I ate pancake batter for my meal of the day because it was cheap and filling.

Off My Knees

A few days later, my lawyer called and told me the date and court where I would be sentenced. That night, I heard the melodious clanging of the bells on nearby boats, and tried to go to sleep.

I knew I was going to prison.

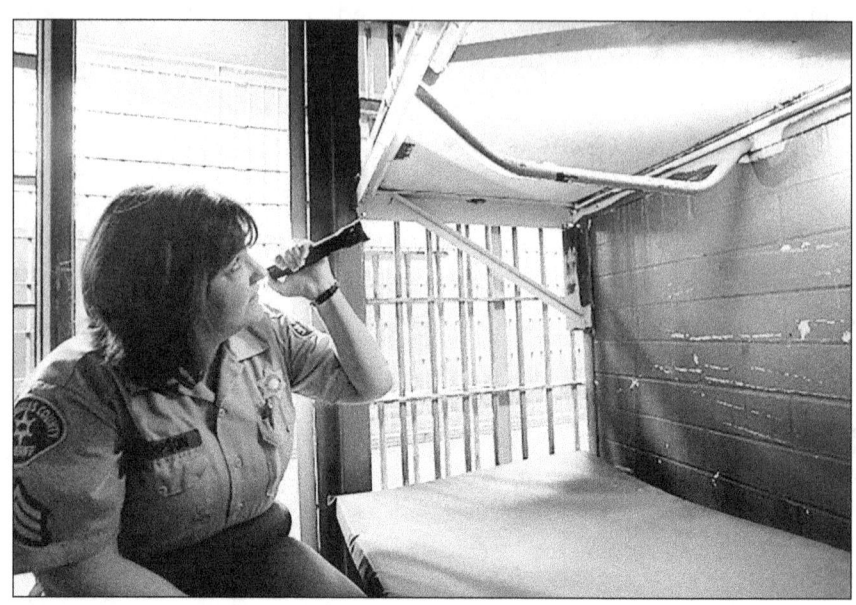

Deputy Inspecting Jail Cel Sybil Brand
(Bars, used when inmates killed themselves, later removed)

Cell Block, Sybil Brand

Chapter Seven

PRISON AND PAROLE

Guilty.
In January 1983, with my attorney beside me, I listened as the charge was read. The charge, civil code 476A, was for writing checks with insufficient funds against my own account. I was guilty and that was how I answered.

The judge, a Black man whose name was Loren Miller Jr., looked at me with kindness in his eyes.

"You have come awfully far down," he said.

He sentenced me to sixteen months, my term to be served at California Rehabilitation Center, or CRC, a state women's prison in a town called Norco.

I knew deep inside me that if I did not go to prison, I would die. Die because my drug-ravaged body was on the verge of collapse. After years of drug abuse and criminal behavior, I had hit bottom.

When I reported to prison a week later, Jules drove me to the intake building in Los Angeles. I was thirty-six years old and facing the unknown of prison time.

"Keep your eyes open and your mouth shut," Jules told me.

Without looking back, I clenched my teeth and got out of the car. I walked up a sidewalk to the entrance of what looked like an old office building. My attorney had told me to take a few toiletries and a small bag of extra clothing to wear when I was in prison.

Walking into a large room, I saw women sitting on wooden benches, most with a small suitcase beside them. I took a seat on the bench and as I waited, I lowered my head and gazed at the old wooden floor. I felt numb as I waited for the next step.

The hours passed slowly.

"Come on, let's go outside and have a smoke," a woman seated on the bench beside me said. "We're allowed as long as we stay inside the courtyard."

A group of us gathered, smoking one cigarette after another. Some of the women had done time before. We eagerly asked them questions, looking to them for knowledge of prison life, anxious for any bit of information.

"Summers, this way," a woman called out.

I was led to a small office for intake.

"Do you use drugs?" my intake manager asked me in a professional voice.

"No," I replied, remembering the advice of my attorney not to mention drug use or the Hell's Angels.

"Do you know any gang members?"

"No."

My answers determined where I would spend my time, and who my dorm mates would be.

She assigned me the number W18047, never to be forgotten.

The bus ride from intake in Los Angeles to the prison in Norco took over two hours. There was little talking. The smell of cows permeated the bus, growing stronger as we got closer to the prison. Norco was cow country and the feeling of being immersed in the smell of cow gas and manure was almost overwhelming.

Located east of Los Angeles in the city of Norco, California Rehabilitation Center or CRC had been built in 1929 as the Lake Norconian Resort, a hotel for the rich and famous. An opulent playground for some of Hollywood's biggest names, it lasted less than a decade before going out of business. After the attack on Pearl Harbor, the property was deeded to the Navy for use as a hospital until 1957.

In 1963 the property was turned over to the state and became a combined prison and drug treatment center. The buildings had rolling hills surrounding them, and a man-made lake. The prison was a series of long, flat buildings that looked like college dorms, surrounded by cement walkways and trees.

When we arrived at the facility, we were told to enter through the back doors. I was about to find out there was a lot of personal freedom. Guards were not constantly present, and I was able to go unescorted to wherever I was supposed to be.

"Get off the bus, go straight, and into the first building you see," the guard directed us.

"You'll receive your dorm assignment, a pillow, sheets, and blanket."

On my way to the dorm I saw the shower room. It was big, with shower-heads lined up in a row high on the wall, giving no privacy. Toilet stalls, which did give privacy, lined the room. I later found out we could only use the showers at assigned times, but had free use of the toilets.

Walking into the dorm, I saw that the women were dressed as they would be on the outside. Some had on makeup. There were sixteen bunk beds. The floor was gray linoleum and everything was very clean. We each had our own locker, clean sheets once a week, and fresh towels every three days. I longed for a washcloth.

∴

"Hi, I'm Yogi," said the woman in the bunk next to mine.
"Julie," I replied.

The room belonged to Yogi. She was short in stature but she was a smooth powerhouse. A mixture of Mexican and Chinese heritages, she was very cute. And boy, was she a charmer. She even had the guards charmed. She told us she was in for pimping and pandering, but we never got any details.

She always had a crowd of girls around her. I watched in fascination and spoke little. In nighttime conversations, when we were in our bunks, I did have the wherewithal to say I was under the protection of the Hell's Angels, providing just enough detail to be believed.

Yogi acknowledged my presence, and depending on the conversation, gave short replies, saying, "Hey girlfriend, what do you think of this?" or "What it be like?," "I'm not the one," and "I'm scared of you!, the last said in a joking manner.

Being around Yogi began to have an effect on me. I was intrigued by the way she handled everyone around her. She made me feel as if I belonged to the group in the dorm. It felt good interacting with others. We all had our flaws, but we got along together.

So when Yogi asked me to stand watch while she and a few others got high on heroin, of course I gladly did so. To block the guard's view, I put the ironing board at the front of the dorm, positioning it and myself to partially obstruct the sitting guard's view into our room. I made a good decoy. At worst, I could have been written up for an infraction and done more time.

There was a lot of drug use at this facility. I saw someone "kick" heroin cold turkey. Walking down the hallway, a woman dropped in front of us, kicking the cement with her legs as hard as she could.

"She's kickin'! She's kickin!" someone yelled.

"Get sugar. Get sugar. Get all the sugar you can."

It did not matter who the woman was or who her enemies were, everyone understood that she needed help right now. We made a circle around her and kept her from banging her head on the cement. Women brought candy bars and cookies. As the more experienced inmates came, I was pushed to the back of the circle and then out.

Watching and hearing someone kick heroin cold turkey was a horrible experience. It gave me chills up and down my back, then around my neck. Staying with me for a long time, her cries sounded like someone who has seen hell.

I went back to my bunk and wrote this poem:

MONKEY ON MY BACK

Step right up, folks, and watch this monkey ride a man,
My little friend the monkey has me holding out my hand.

He climbs higher on my shoulders for all the world
  to see,
But as they laugh, they fail to know, this weight is
  killing me.

Gone are all the smiles he once put on my face,
Instead upon my shoulders, he's left a morphine trace.

Of all that's fed this monkey, he never can be full;
Searching for one more illusion, on my bones he starts
  to pull.
Standing on the corner, in my hand will come a pack,
Of morphine-powdered illusions for this monkey on
  my back.

∴∴

    Although I didn't realize it, I was tested in other ways. During rest period, when women wanted to have sex, they let the room know and then had sex in the bunk next to mine. I could hear the raw, squishy sounds they made, but I lay quietly in my bed and minded my own business.

    Most of the women were ten or more years younger than me. Through the eyes of the other inmates, I was an old woman of thirty-six and not much of a threat. I had no gang affiliations, no axes to grind, no battles to fight. I saw women who stood little chance of succeeding in life. Many were from low-income families. Their lifestyle and lack of education and opportunity were heavy burdens.

    I did not see "good" or "bad," but saw many women who had been arrested for the pettiest of crimes, done county jail time, were released, arrested again, and sent to state prison. It is not up to me to judge, and I did not judge.

• •
• •

When it was mealtime, we walked, dorm by dorm, to the cafeteria. We were free to walk and eat with whomever we wanted. The meals were tasty and plentiful, full of starch and sugar.

"Donkey dicks, donkey dicks, we're having donkey dicks tonight," we joked, referring to the large sausage for dinner. Other nights, we had "mystery meat." My bunkmates who worked in the cafeteria used to smuggle cookies back to the dorm. I gained a good fifty pounds.

• •
• •

During intake, I had been asked where I would like to work.

"I would like to work in the yard," I replied.

I knew I did not want to work in the laundry or kitchen. I thought fresh air and exercise would help my body get strength back. I was the only yard worker from my dorm, and left at 8:45 a.m. for the short walk to meet with twenty or so other yard workers, each from a different dorm. When we met at the assigned place, the person in charge gave us our duties for the day, usually two people at a time.

"Come on, we have to pull the weeds in the flowerbeds in front of the admin building," a girl called out to me.

After a short walk to the admin building, rake and hoe in hand, I tried to be productive. But I was too weak to do the job, so I leaned on the rake, pretending to work. We were paid seven cents an hour. The amount was put on our intake books that kept track of the money we earned and the money sent to us by people on the outside.

⁂

CRC provided group sessions that were attempts at rehabilitation. One evening a month we were sent to a room with about twenty other women. Standing up in a circle, we put our arms on each other's shoulders. Going from person to person, it became my turn. "I am a thief," I said. That really hit home and grounded it for me.

Returning to my dorm, I looked into the prison chapel, which was always open. I looked in, then walked by. I wasn't ready for God's help.

⁂

We were allowed weekly phone calls. I called either Jules or E.J., always collect. On a call with Jules, I begged him to send me money.

"Jules, please, please put some of my money on my books," I begged during a telephone call.

He eventually did. That cash, along with the money I earned from working in the yard, added up to what I could spend at the canteen. When I knew I had money on my books, I walked, at the allowed time, to a small room and was given my ducats, the prison slang word for money. The ducats were small pieces of paper, with an amount on them, corresponding to money. Then I returned to the dorm and put the ducats in my locker, secured with a combination lock.

Canteen night began early on Friday evenings. The canteen was a small room with the top half of the door open, and a shelf on the closed bottom half. Leaning against the shelf, I looked at the toiletries, soda, and candy lining the back shelves. Tampax and sanitary pads had to be bought at canteen and were the most expensive. Due to my drug use, my period had stopped. It would resume years later, but this meant I could spend my ducats on what I wanted.

"Please give me three Snickers bars and two Hershey's bars," I requested.

Back in my room, I always asked my bunkmates if they wanted some. Then I promptly ate what was left, never saving any.

Jules sent me a package. He forgot the washcloth but put in big bags of candy, which I shared around the dorm. In that same box was a pair of white tennis shoes that I wanted so badly. I felt elated when I put them on. How good they felt. Then looking around, I saw how many women did not have this luxury. Some had small children at home. I began to realize that I came from a privileged background.

∷

Saturday mornings were "Double Scrub" time. We always griped when we were assigned a location in either the shower room or the dorm. But we scrubbed every inch of every surface within an inch of its life. This took aggression out of the women who did the scrubbing, and gave us pride in our dorm.

On Saturday evenings we could sign up for the weekly dance activity. In 1983 Michael Jackson's "Thriller" was at the top of the charts, and the atmosphere of the dance room was happy. I wanted to dance with Yogi, and never did because I was too shy to ask her. She knew I had a crush on her and I did not go to the dances often.

On Sundays, a guard stood in the doorframe of our room to deliver our mail. Holding up a bundle, she called out the inmate's name.

"Mail, Summers."

The guard never entered our room. The mail was passed down from one inmate to another until it reached the recipient.

The guard's announcement meant I had a letter from E.J., who wrote often. My contact with the outside world was limited. I heard nothing from either of my brothers. Once I had a picture taken that could be sent home. This cost a dollar. I saved my money so that I could send it to E.J.

On our next phone call all she did was cry. "But honey, I couldn't recognize you."

It upset her to see that I had gotten heavy, my teeth had fallen out and my hair was thin and dark, not my usual bleached blonde. Knowing E.J., she ripped up the picture.

∴

Sunday afternoon was visiting day, and Jules came to see me a few times.

"Visit, Summers!" the guard called out one Sunday morning.

I knew to look forward to seeing him that afternoon.

Visits were held in a supervised area outside in a yard with picnic benches and water coolers for those inmates who had family bringing food. It was a great break in the monotony.

But my visits with Jules were awkward.

"My Lord, this is such a long ride here to see you for an hour," Jules grumbled. "And you look terrible anyway. I am not sending you any more candy."

On our return from the visiting area we were given a body cavity search. Mine was visual because I had not admitted to using drugs during my intake. Getting naked, and being told to "Bend over, spread 'em, squat, and cough," was a small price to pay for the break in routine.

⁙

A large woman jumped me outside in the yard. Her name was Brenda and she was not from my dorm. She claimed she had read my jacket, my intake file, and that I was a snitch. A snitch is right under a baby killer in the prison hierarchy of bad people and meant I would be frozen out from the inmates and a target for anyone who wanted to take out their frustrations.

"Liar, liar," I screamed at her, getting angrier by the minute.

"Fight, fight!" was called and the girls gathered around us. I fought as tough and as dirty as I could, throwing dirt at her eyes and broken tree branches at her. I punched her everywhere I could, with most of my punches landing in her big, blubbery stomach. She did not put up much of a fight, we were not hurt, and I was the winner, so she left me alone. I never found out why she did that.

⁙

I had a really good birthday in my prison cell. A few of my bunkmates worked in the kitchen. They took food, paper, and matches and brought them to the dorm. Someone stood guard as they rolled back a mattress and built a small fire on the bedsprings.

They cooked something good for me, singing, "Every party needs a pooper, that's why we invited you, party pooper."

That said something about my personality. But they could have done some serious time for their infractions, so I knew I was liked and accepted.

⁙

I was assigned a counselor to help me with the transition to my new life when I was released.

"Summers, follow me. Now," my counselor called out. Seating me on a chair next to his desk, he told me my customhouse broker's license had been revoked.

My devastation must have shown in my face.

"Well, what did you expect?" he said flatly.

I was bummed out for a long time. This closed a big door for me. When I got out of prison, I wouldn't be able to work in a business where I had experience and success. I would be forced to find other ways to support myself. When my counselor asked me questions about my plans once I had served my sentence, I realized I didn't have any.

⁙

At night my bunkmates and I crossed each day off our mental calendars. We talked about never coming back, but I heard them talk and realized the recidivism rate is high. Once a felon is back on the street, it's easy for the police to bust them for the least infraction. It becomes a vicious cycle, a way of life.

I had a new plan and talked to my bunkmates about finding a man to mentor me. I knew he would want a good looker and felt I needed plastic surgery done to accomplish this. The ravages of drug use and prison time had taken their toll on me, and E.J. had shown me the way, getting her face and breasts done when she worked for me.

⁙

After doing eight months of time on my sixteen-month sentence, I was eligible for parole.

I knew E.J. was living with someone she did not know well and there was no room for me. My brother Don had recently married and was living with his new wife in Indiana. I had no one else.

Jules was my last resort. When I asked him if I could parole to his house, he agreed. Knowing I would be at his sexual mercy, it sounded like pure hell. But who would take me to live with them just for myself? Such was my self-esteem.

My release date came at the end of September 1983. The State gave each inmate two hundred dollars upon release. I promptly sent one hundred to E.J.

∷

My last prison bus ride was to a halfway house located in a rundown part of downtown Los Angeles. Halfway houses are designed to help former prisoners adjust to being back in society. It is required by the state before a convict can parole. It also serves as a residence. Mine turned out to be an old apartment building. It was dirty and had the neglected smell of too many people.

Assigned to a room with one other woman, I seldom saw her. Men and women had their own sides of the building with the toilet and showers at the end of the hall.

We had freedom during the day, and were able to check in and out with the person at the front desk. I kept to myself, sometimes smoking with the others in an open side yard.

"I'm going for a job interview, Dan," I said to the man at the front desk as I checked out for the day. Instead of looking for work, I just walked around the city with nowhere to go. One of my teeth started really hurting. I sat down on the street curb, crying. A tall Black man came up behind me and asked, "What's the matter?"

I told him my tooth hurt.

"I am a dentist. Do you want me to pull it for you?" he said in a very concerned voice.

"Yes," I said. I followed him to his office.

This man asked for no payment in return for helping me with my tooth, and his kindness stays with me to this day.

∷

As my release date got closer, I was called into the parole officer's office. I sat on a chair across the desk from him as he asked me questions about where I would be staying during my parole. I gave Jules's address in the Hollywood Hills.

"Oh, I have always wanted to go to a house in the Hollywood Hills," he said, his voice filled with awe.

In that moment, I saw the power of money. I knew that I was the same person if I paroled to Hollywood Hills or a poor part of town, but the parole officer did not.

I also knew that being in this house would look good from the outside, but living inside it was another story.

∷

"Denny's it is. How does that sound?" Jules asked me when he picked me up.

"Fine," I said in a glum voice. After two months in the halfway house, I was hoping to eat in a much grander place for my first meal.

My new ex-con persona was a great disappointment to Jules. When I was on speed, I was very thin, almost emaciated. I had dressed well, fixed my hair, and of course, talked a lot. Now, I was half dead, and looked and acted it.

It was hard to take any pleasure living in such a nice house. I had my own bedroom and bath, but I had to sleep in Jules's bed at night. He wanted me in his life because he needed sex. While nice-looking physically, Jules had bad body odor due to a medical condition. And the thirty-year age difference meant our sex life was not the best.

Jules was impotent. I worked and worked at trying to get an erection on him, but it was in vain. He decided to get a penile implant, probably one of the first. A bulb attached to the outside of the penis was supposed to inflate the implant inside his penis. I squeezed and squeezed that bulb, but it did not work. These attempts continued throughout the day.

Wiping the spittle from the corners of his mouth, as older people sometimes do, he sickened me when he constantly tried to have sex. There is little worse for a woman than having to submit to a man when she does not want to.

He got to me, doing something as simple as sucking on my nipples. On the day he did that I could not put up a wall between him and the feeling that he was taking my essence from me. When I say prostitution rips out the soul, it is this feeling, the feeling that I cannot protect what is mine, the deepest part of me. When this is taken by a man, pulled out of a woman, there is nothing left. The woman is a shell.

∷

A few months after going to Jules's house, I was taking a shower when a stream of black, foul-smelling liquid came out of my anus. It ran down my legs and into the drain. This happened several times, but I did not tell Jules or go to the doctor. Years later

I realized it was blood and I must have been bleeding internally. It would be a long time until I got my strength back.

I was in pain, and Jules had a well-stocked medicine cabinet, so I helped myself to what was in it. He had a good supply of Ativan and Valium for anxiety; codeine number three and four for pain. The painkillers Percodan and Percocet were my favorites.

Whenever I went out, I returned on a bus that left me at the corner near the bottom of the hill.

"Walk up the hill after you get off the bus. I'm not coming down to get you," Jules told me. "It will be good for you."

That hill was a challenge. I had to stop and rest constantly. Jules finally agreed to lend me five hundred dollars so that I could buy a car.

I bought an old blue Fiat and began looking for a job. Jules wouldn't buy me any clothes. I wanted one new outfit to go to job interviews, so I found a thrift shop.

Occasionally I would steal twenty dollars from Jules's wallet until it made one hundred dollars and then send it to E.J. I despised Jules, maybe even hated him a little. When we were in bed watching TV, he'd ask me about the drug dealers I knew. He told me told me he would put up the front money to go into business with them, saying we would make a lot of money. I knew not to go near this.

∷

How did I integrate myself back into the world? I watched TV. I watched the news and different programs and the world started to gradually filter in. When I watched violent movies, I would try to feel something. My mind was scrambled and my body, still feeling the effects of meth use, hurt badly all over. I could not remember the simplest things and could not put two and two together.

One day I looked in the mirror and saw a very old woman with vacant eyes. This frightened me. I knew then that I would have to look and act and dress a certain way so that I could pass as a normal person. I would make a life.

∷

I got a job as a chip girl in a casino on the outskirts of Los Angeles in Gardena.

"Come to my house after work. We will have some fun," said a man I had seen several times at the gambling tables.

We went back to his place where we snorted meth and had sex. But it did not feel right. I knew I had to get back to Jules's house so I could go to work the next day.

A few months later, I quit the casino job and found a position at Briareus, a computer software company. Jobs were easy to get and of course I did not check the box that asked if I had ever been arrested.

I liked my job, working hard as a dispatcher, scheduling repairmen and customers for repair work on the computer systems we provided. This was a big step up for me. I began sending E.J. two hundred and fifty dollars a month, and would do this for the rest of her life.

Driving home one afternoon, I stopped at a 7-Eleven.

"Are you Phyllis Diller, the comedienne?" the clerk asked, very sincerely.

Because the comedienne was a good twenty-five years older than me, this encounter made me begin to think longer and harder about how to improve my appearance. Although I had lost weight and gotten my figure back, I still needed help.

Dentistry and plastic surgery were covered under my insurance plan at work. I asked a co-worker for his recommendation for a dentist, and hit the jackpot when I found Dr. Dashut. His copays were almost nonexistent.

"I like doing the work on you," he told me.

Dr. Dashut spent many hours filling cavities, doing root canals, and replacing my broken teeth with caps. He did a beautiful job. After years of not having teeth, I was elated.

∷

In 1985, I was thirty-eight. Although I was very young for plastic surgery, I had a tough girl look that showed where I had been. And deep in my memory were times from my childhood when company came to the house, looked at me, and said, "She will never be as pretty as her mother."

When I asked Dr. Dashut if he knew of a good plastic surgeon, he referred me to one of his close friends, Dr. Steven Gottlieb, who was just starting practice in Beverly Hills.

I did not plan on multiple surgeries, but Dr. Gottlieb took a liking to me. He did one operation, then another, again with minimal copays. By now my health had stabilized and I was a good patient.

On my first visit to him, Dr. Gottlieb asked, "How did you get this scar on your nose?" I lied and told him I had gone through the front windshield in a car crash, but remembered how I had caused it myself during my meth days.

Driving home, I felt a deep warmth settle over my shoulders and encircle my back, lasting several minutes. I felt like God had his arms around me. Profoundly overcome by this feeling, I made a promise to God that I would use my newfound beauty only for good and never for ill-gotten gain.

The results were astonishing. Over a two-year period, I had an eyelift, cheek implants, nose reduction, a facelift, and breast implants. I was lucky. Dr. Gottlieb had the gift of creating beauty. My face began to settle in. I was a pretty woman, and looked much younger than my age.

People began to treat me differently. In stores and restaurants people fell all over themselves to give me good service. It was difficult for me to process this. People thought because I was pretty on the outside, I must be pretty on the inside.

It's very subtle, the way we perceive others when there is no major introduction. We look at the face, skin, hair color, nails, and style of clothing, including shoes. We then treat people according to what we perceive. I inherently knew that and changed my appearance accordingly. Above all, I wanted to fit in.

And I was looking for that man, the one who would mentor me.

* *
* *

The days at Jules's house were not all bad. We both loved music and many Saturdays we went to orchestral concerts around the city. But on the Sundays, when he took me to his boat, it was hard work. The boat, named *Second Fiddle*, was docked in Marina del Rey and was a fifty-foot Kettenburg sailboat, made of all wood.

"Come on, Julie. Today we're cleaning the cabin from top to bottom," came from Jules.

Other times, at his instruction, I climbed to the top of the twenty-five-foot mast and sanded it with sandpaper, starting where I had previously left off. I became exhausted well before the end of the day. He never took me sailing, and looking back, I think he took other women.

I kept a notebook of Jules's many ways of saving money.

"Tear the paper towels in four pieces, Julie, and only use one square at a time."

"You have a toothache? Soak some cotton in a solution of clove, and put it on the tooth." I lost that tooth.

"Your car is having radiator problems? Here's a two-gallon jug. Fill it with water and carry it in the car. If you're on the freeway, pull over and let the car cool down."

"Only use the front burner on the stove. It takes less electricity."

E.J. and I had many laughs over this, but it was not fun to live with.

"What can you possibly talk about for so long?" was Jules's usual question to me after I got off the phone with E.J.

We talked about anything and everything, as if to make up for lost time. E.J. had not done well after leaving Costa Mesa. Then one day during a phone call she said, "Please pray for me, honey, I have nowhere to go and I have applied to HUD for government-subsidized housing."

Housing and Urban Development ran a building in Orlando with subsidized apartments for low-income people. We were both elated when she got a place she could afford to live.

I visited E.J. during the summer and over Christmas at her HUD apartment, paying the airfare from my salary at work. We took great delight in our visits, constantly talking, and occasionally going to dinner.

When I visited E.J., I saw things that went into my subconscious, to surface later. Once I would have considered the people who lived in HUD housing poor and beneath me. But I saw E.J. gratefully eat cheese, or whatever was available from the food given by welfare, and I began to see the other residents, people just like me, who were thankful for a place to live, and respected one another. They had been given back their dignity. This had a great effect on me and would influence me in later life, making me an advocate of those with little income.

∷

Then came the fateful call. It was E.J., and she said, "I have pancreatic cancer, and I am getting an operation to try and get the cancer out." I did not know what to say. Fear ran through me. I knew the word cancer but I did not realize that the survival rate for pancreatic cancer was usually short.

I did not have enough money saved, and Jules would not lend me the money for airfare to go see E.J. Although I resented it terribly then, in retrospect it was probably the best thing.

Because she was a favorite among the tenants where she lived, the other tenants put their names on a sheet of paper kept at the front desk, asking to be the next in line to take her to the doctor. Her next-door neighbor nursed her. I knew she was well taken care of.

∷

After work, on my way home to Jules, I routinely stopped in at Le Dome, a high-class restaurant on Sunset Boulevard, sat at the bar, and had a drink. One of the regulars was a man named Buddy. After several conversations, I told him how unhappy I was living with Jules.

"I know a young, beautiful French actress named Lydie who's looking for a roommate," Buddy said. "Let me introduce you."

He said he would help me if I wanted to move in with her. I happily said yes. Then he offered me a job in his office where he worked in the new QVC television sales market.

The move-out from Jules's house was fast. I had paid him back for the loan on my car and had few possessions.

Jules was recently honored by a famous fellow architect, John Lautner. Mr. Lautner named a home in Echo Park that he found and restored, calling it the "Jules Salkin Residence." Jules was a fascinating man, but I did not appreciate my time with him.

But I am eternally grateful that he gave me a place to live when I had no place else to go.

California Rehabilitation Center (CRC)

Entrance to California Rehabilitation Center

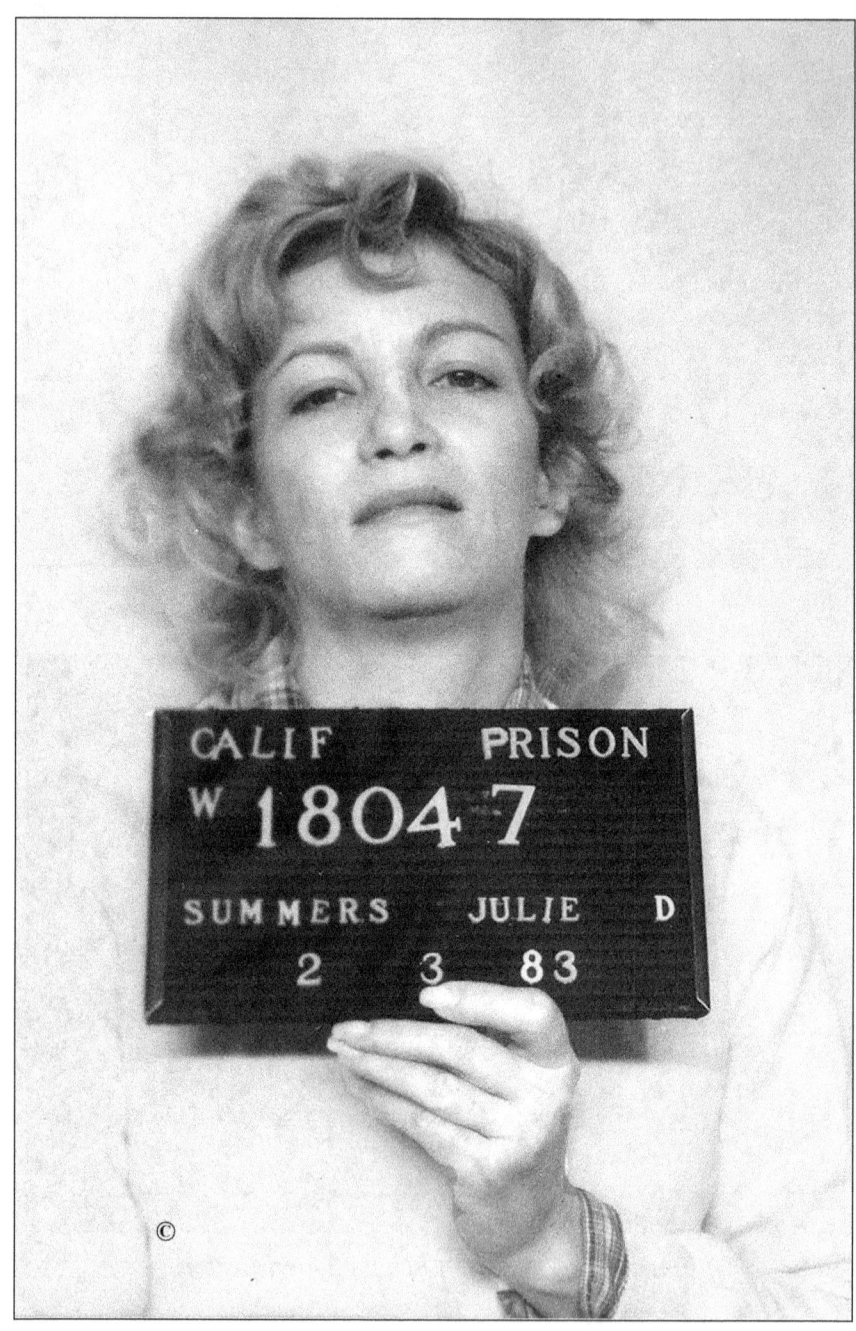

Prison Mugshot

Jules Salkin

Jules and I

Julie D. Summers

Coming Out of Jule's Boat

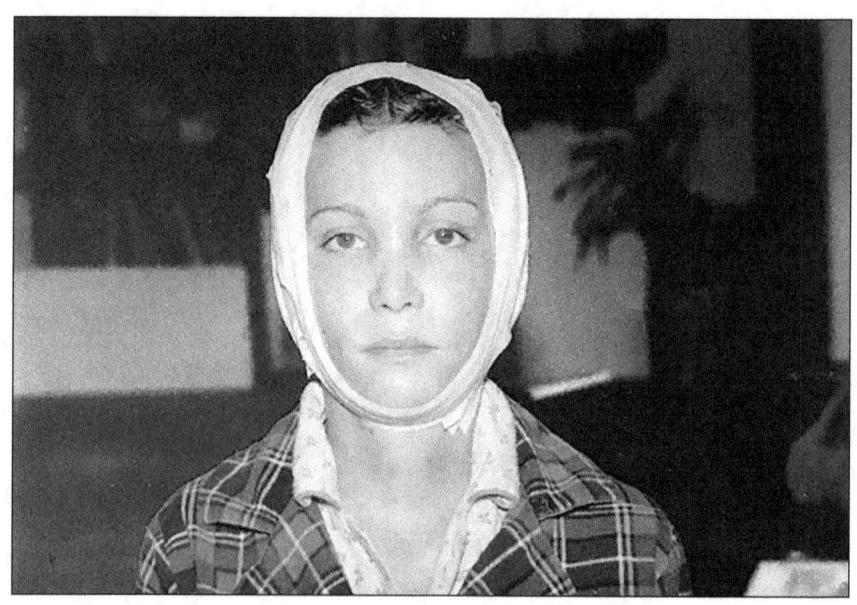

In Bandages from Facelift

Chapter Eight

MEETING ARIS ANAGNOS, AND E.J.'S DEATH

The move-in with Lydie, my new roommate, was fast too. I liked her the moment I met her. She lived in a 200-unit apartment building on Franklin Avenue, which was convenient to everything.

Buddy's company was at the forefront in selling products on TV. I enjoyed working for him in the office, but I wanted more freedom and the ability to make more money. Buddy and I agreed to split the profit I made on imitation French perfume outside the office, and I began selling the perfume at swap meets and flea markets, making the circuit of Los Angeles and Orange County.

Working in swap meets was not easy. I had to get up at four in the morning, wait in line to enter the location, then begin the day. Finding a spot, unpacking the bottles, then standing in the hot sun all day behind the display table was hard work. I did this for almost a year. But another big change in my life was near.

"Come, we are moving to a condo on Hollywood Boulevard. It is beautiful and you will love it," Lydie said in her enchanting

French accent. "The same man who owns this building also owns that one."

But Lydie and I were not there long when she missed a rent payment. "The owner is coming tomorrow to show the condo to a woman who wants to buy it," she told me.

Opening the front door the next morning, I met the owner. In a scene that was almost surreal, I saw a glow of lavender surrounding him. As he entered the condo, he took my hand, stepped inside, then said a quick hello as he and his client did a walk-through of the apartment.

His secretary called the next day and asked if I would like to rent a single apartment back at Franklin Avenue. I said yes, then Lydie and I said goodbye. Soon after settling into my apartment in the new building, I was walking through the lobby to get my mail, and there stood the owner. I saw a man, a beautiful man, who looked like a Greek God. He wore a cream-colored suit with a white shirt. The sun shone on him. Even his salt-and-pepper hair glistened.

"My name is Aris Anagnos," he said in a deep multi-accented voice. Later I learned he spoke, read, and wrote six languages fluently. Handsome as any movie star, his demeanor was courtly and cultured.

Maybe it was the way I looked at him or maybe he had looked at my rental application and knew I was single. But when he called a few weeks later and asked if I would like him to visit me, I could feel the heat of his intention.

Wearing a new aqua outfit that made me look tan and thin, I answered the door and invited him in. Wasting no time, Aris said, "Come and lie down with me, Julie."

We sat on my bed, a mattress on the floor, and he unbuttoned the top of my blouse, peering down the valley of my perfect plastic surgery breasts.

When I looked into his eyes, the color of the rolling ocean, and breathed in his smell of his lavender soap and Paco Rabanne cologne, I felt all of his masculinity and charisma.

Slowly he continued unbuttoning my blouse, then stood up and without a word began taking off his clothes. He then joined me in taking off the remainder of my clothes. We made love and it was wonderful. It was more wonderful because he was rich. This was the man I had manifested before I left prison.

After a few months, Aris began giving me spending money. When I told him I was working swap meets and my car was having problems, he gave me five thousand dollars in cash. After he left, I threw the money up in the air in celebration.

"Whoopee!" I cheered.

The hundred-dollar bills went all over the room. After calling E.J. to give her the news, I did it again.

∷

My job with Buddy became part-time, and soon Buddy faded from my life.

When Aris visited me at my apartment, it was all about sex. I did not talk much, instinctively knowing that I was in the presence of a very powerful and important person. The visits became more frequent.

When Aris asked if I would like to move into a condo in yet another one of his buildings and not pay rent, I felt like I had won the lottery. Imagine, not having to pay rent.

"May I have drapes instead of blinds?" I asked him.

When he said yes, I felt as if I were truly rich.

Everything felt right to me except that he was married to his third wife, who was in poor health. Letting me know he had two grown children by a former wife, he honorably told me nothing would change his status quo. In spite of this, I started to fall in love with him.

∷

Aris knew how badly I wanted to visit E.J. in Florida, so he gave me the money to go often. E.J.'s and my visits became more personal than they had been. At long last, she explained the rage inside her that came from the early sexual molestation by her foster father. In one of our conversations, she revealed the abuse she had suffered.

"When I was thirteen or fourteen he started raping me. He raped me all the time." She sobbed into her handkerchief as she turned away from me, her shoulders hunched over.

"I hated myself because sometimes I enjoyed the sex," she confessed.

This information was new and upsetting to me. It helped explain my mother's erratic moods and behavior. She had been emotionally damaged by her mother's early abandonment and death, and she was helpless when her foster father abused her.

E.J. now took a stand for the first time in her life.

"I am never going to talk with Gram again."

And she never did. Gram was now living with my brother Robert and his wife Sherry in Montana. When E.J. had a phone conversation with Gram and told her about the abuse, Gram denied any knowledge of her husband's molestation. The family split.

Robert and Sherry believed Gram, I believed E.J., and Don remained neutral. This rift in the family would remain.

Off My Knees

∷

In December 1987, E.J. called me. She was sixty-six years old.

"Please, honey, come and stay with me for a while."

I knew something was wrong. When I walked in the door of her apartment, I took one look at her and it flashed in my subconscious that she was dying. But I could not let that thought into my mind.

A year before, E.J. and I had taken a walk past the local hospital. Looking up at it, she said, "I am going to die there."

I knew she had a great fear of hospitals and said, "Don't talk like that."

She replied, "I do not want to die in a hospital."

My brother Don, his wife Maribeth, and their six-month-old son, Aaron, arrived from Indianapolis for Christmas. They were able to stay in a nearby motel only a few days. E.J. did her best to entertain the family. Dressed in a new blue top and a nice pair of black slacks that I had given her for Christmas, she sat in her red chair as we gave out presents. Her constant pain pills spoke for her.

"Everything is going by too fast," she said.

After Don and his family left, I decided to stay with E.J. For the next six weeks I did not leave her side. When my brothers called to see how she was doing, my reply was, "There is no change."

∷

Aris called me every morning, making me feel loved and supported, but for the remainder of the day and evening I sat in E.J.'s red chair in the living room with no TV, radio, or books. She did not want to hear any noise so my thoughts were my only company. My mother was my reason for living and all I knew was how much I loved her.

Sometimes I went to the kitchenette and sobbed into a towel, quietly and desperately. Then I returned to my chair, her red chair.

At night, when she went to the bathroom, she threw up vomit and fecal matter. It went all over everything, the toilet, the floor, the walls, the smell mixing in with the new, cheap plastic pink shower curtain that she had so proudly bought. I too threw up when, later, I scrubbed everything down. Then I went back to my mattress on the floor beside her bed, taking Xanax and Ambien together to sleep.

E.J.'s doctor called, recommending hospice. The doctor sent someone from the hospice organization to talk to E.J. and me about what to do next. We listened, but E.J. soon dismissed them.

When I sat on her bed and held her hand, we looked at each other, not needing the words to say I love you. Sometimes she wanted water or food, but most of the time she just lay in her bed, dying.

∷

One evening the Florida rain came pouring down. Standing in the living room and looking out of the gray window at the rain and trees, I felt the warmth of God for the second time, His arm around my shoulders. The feeling was warm, peaceful, loving, calm, and blissful. Feeling comforted, I knew God was with me.

There is an energy that comes from the darkness. I won't call it the devil, but it is palpable. I think we can call on this energy and feel a certain black power from it. I know I had been doing so for years, and in that moment I felt the difference between good and evil, lightness and dark, and thank goodness, the energy of the light was greater to me.

Then E.J. made a funny sound. There was a difference in her breathing. I called her doctor, who said it sounded like she had a small stroke.

A little later, E.J.'s next door neighbor, Esther, came in to visit. Esther had taken care of E.J. after her surgery, and I explained to her what had just happened.

"This is enough, she must go to the hospital," Esther told me. "Pack a small bag so you can stay with her," she told me.

Esther drove us to the hospital. Fright gripped my heart, but I still could not comprehend that E.J. was dying.

Once she was put into her room, E.J. and I sat side by side on her hospital bed, our legs dangling over the side, holding hands. Full of trust and love, we said the Lord's Prayer together. Those were the last words E.J. spoke. Shortly after lying down on the bed, she slid into a coma.

Like a mother hen, I stood guard over her and did not leave the room. I had a cot to sleep on, and my meals were sent in with hers. I called my brother with the news of E.J.'s condition.

"She is still in a coma, Don." I spoke in quiet and hushed tones on the telephone. I knew E.J. could still hear me.

∴

A few days later Don arrived. On my way to pick him up at the airport, E.J. died. It was January 23, 1988.

Don and I arrived back at her hospital room to the sight of nurses putting E.J.'s body into a heavy, black body bag. I shuddered at the sound of the heavy metal zipper closing.

"Do you want to donate her eyes?" one of the nurses asked. Don said no, which was right. E.J. would not have liked that.

Returning to E.J.'s apartment, Don and I put masking tape on the floor, dividing it into three sections: his, mine, and to give away. Touching something once, Don and I had a brief discussion about where the item should go. Taking many Xanax, I tried to work fast to keep out the pain, and we finished before dawn. Don returned to his family the next day.

The people living in the HUD building, E.J.'s friends and neighbors, took a collection to help with expenses. They handed me an envelope filled with money they could barely spare. I was so touched by the sight of the dollar bills that they had collected for their friend.

"Do you want me to call the church and make arrangements for the service here in Orlando?" Esther asked me. I gratefully said yes.

Mama had an open casket. She was dressed in the new blue top she had worn on Christmas day. The great pain she had suffered throughout her illness showed in her pale and pinched face, unable to be erased by embalming. Her body was sent to Pennsylvania for burial.

∴

"Do you need money, Julie?" Aris asked me on the next phone call. He paid for all the funeral arrangements and my airline flight. He also paid for some of her furniture to be shipped to me in Los Angeles.

When I packed for my trip from Los Angeles to Orlando, all I took with me was a light blue cotton jacket and tennis shoes. These were the clothes I wore to Pennsylvania. It was freezing cold but nothing could get through to me.

After the brief service, a man came running after me. "Are you E.J.'s daughter? I had such a crush on her in high school," he said.

When Daddy died, Mama had purchased a burial plot for four people in the cemetery of Good Shepherd Church, the church of my childhood. She was buried there with Daddy, in Meadville, among the many generations of our family.

It's impossible for me to remember any other details of Mama's burial. After the service, I sat at a bar and had a drink with my brother Robert at the Meadville Inn. On my flight home to California, one of the stewardesses asked me if I was okay. I remember her kindness, but little else. Maybe that's because I got as many refills of E.J.'s prescriptions as I could before I left Florida. And of course, I took all the pills on her bedside with me. Percoset, Percodan, codeine number three and four, Ambien, Xanax, pills that I was using to keep out the pain. When I got home, it finally hit me that she had died.

∴∴

I did not send her quietly to her afterlife. I knew from an early morning phone call when Aris would visit, so I sobered up before he came in the late afternoon. The rest of the time I took pills, never knowing how many, and washed them down with peach brandy.

When I woke up, I cried into the mattress. If I went to the kitchen, I put my head on the countertop and sobbed. I had loved my mother with all my heart and soul, just as she had loved me. I felt like she was the last person on Earth who did love me.

"I give up, I give up, I have lost everything I ever cared about," I wailed to God.

I cried myself sick for many weeks, then the weeks grew into months. I had loved E.J. as if she were not only my mother but my sister, my child, my best friend. I felt that God had taken away the most important person in my life. Now life meant nothing.

Time did not help my grief.

"You win, God, you win," I cried. I do not know what I meant by that. Then I had a feeling of minor rapture, of feeling absolutely pure, and very close to God.

It was almost too pure; I could not tell a little white lie, or say or do anything wrong. I felt heaven, and heaven was inside of me. This feeling, although lasting many months, gradually faded as I continued to drink, smoke, and use pills. But it did not leave entirely.

∷

My life with Aris began to grow stronger. He started to call me darling, and began taking me out to dinner. I felt chills and tingles all over at the sound of his voice, when he called and asked, "Darling, are you available this evening?"

Of course I was. I got dressed to look my best. Any restaurant Aris chose had to be of the highest quality, have white tablecloths and a bevy of waiters. At these dinners, I let Aris do all the talking, and gradually learned what a complex and interesting man he was.

As the founder and president of many progressive organizations, he was known and respected both locally, and in foreign countries. In addition to his success as a businessman, he was a philanthropist.

Aris came from a wealthy family in Greece, but when Hitler invaded Greece in 1941, his family lost everything. Aris managed to escape by taking a small boat to Cyprus. He came to the United States with two hundred and fifty dollars in his pocket.

Aris told me that when he was fifty, he decided to make money to support the socialist causes he believed in, and this was how he became a self-made multimillionaire. He knew that people have problems and suffer, and he used his money and power to help people. It was his idealism, his goodness, that made me fall more in love with him.

I adored him and wanted to be just like him. Aris was my world now. His kindness shone out of his eyes, kindness that reflected his survival of the atrocities he had experienced as a young man during World War II.

Slowly, in the soft glow after our lovemaking, Aris asked me questions about my past, making certain he knew the facts, as if he did not want to make a misstep himself.

"Darling, I want you to start reading the newspaper," Aris suggested. He realized I was woefully ignorant of the world. Then he had me go to his office, where I made photocopies and did filing. I got to overhear how he did business, which I found fascinating. He had an appropriate answer for everyone, and handled his business with experience and finesse.

My heart seared with hot pain when he took his wife on two-month vacations to the Caribbean, but he always made sure I had spending money. When he bought me simple presents, a bathmat or a trench coat, my heart melted, thinking of this busy and important man taking the time to go to a department store to buy something he knew I needed.

∴

Gradually, my sorrow at E.J.'s death began to fade, and I began to take fewer pills. I knew better than to become completely dependent on Aris. Years before, E.J. had told me a story of a woman she knew who sat at home all day waiting for the man who was keeping her to call. I was not going to be that person. I collected unemployment, then got a job selling expensive aquariums at a shop on trendy Melrose Avenue.

After about a year, Aris asked me about my plans for my future.

"Darling, why don't you get your real estate license?" he asked.

With his encouragement, I studied real estate books at home for about six months. After my second try, I passed the exam, and when Aris told me to check yes on the box asking if I had a prison record, I did.

"I will pick you up at one o'clock," Aris said. Dressed in his usual silk trousers, short sleeve shirt, and shoes from Italy, Aris went with me to turn in my paperwork to the Department of Real Estate. Calmly and easily, with his power of great persuasion, he talked to the clerk, using just the right words to explain my prison sentence. I got my license.

My real estate career began at Fred Sands Real Estate on Sunset Boulevard, although the only houses I ever sold were the ones Aris sent my way as his referrals.

"Julie, I want to sell my condo, the one you are living in now. Act as the listing agent, and sell it," Aris told me. By selling his condo, and getting more than Aris's expected price, I earned my fee. Then I moved into an apartment in Beverly Hills.

My ego was getting stronger. I believed I could do better at commercial real estate, so I went to work for Bruce Hanes, who was established in selling apartment buildings.

West Hollywood became my assigned area. It took me one year to take pictures of every apartment building of ten units and above in West Hollywood. Pasting the photos on eight-by-ten sheets that went into a binder, I then had to find each building's owner by researching the title, so I could call them. The goal was to talk with the owner and persuade them to sell their building.

I was on commission, my hours were flexible, and I was expected to be in the office much of the day. But I slipped out every afternoon to go home and make love with Aris.

I never sold an apartment building, but I did learn how to manage one.

Aris Anagnos

Aris and I

E.J. and I

E.J. Last Photo

Chapter Nine

THE APARTMENT BUILDING, LIVING IN WEST HOLLYWOOD

"I want you to have freedom, darling. And the way to start is financially," Aris said on one of our afternoon visits. He had walked into my apartment where he saw me working hard at my new endeavor of selling apartment buildings. We started looking at buildings that I could manage.

"No, not that one, darling, it is not big enough," Aris said with his deep, rich laugh, always close to the surface.

A born teacher, Aris began educating me about the construction of buildings.

"Darling, look at how far the windows are spaced apart to know the size of the rooms," he advised.

After a thorough search, we found a good, although run-down, multi-unit building in West Hollywood near the Sunset Strip. Aris bought the building and the deal was done. I moved into a vacant unit so that I could manage the building.

It was 1992, I was forty-five years old, and this was a miracle. I felt safe and pretty and the world was mine. In the nine years since I had left prison, my life had turned around completely. All the efforts I'd made seemed like little steps at the time, but I'd kept moving. I was relieved to be settled with some financial security.

Even though I knew nothing about it, managing the apartment building was a new and exciting job. I set up a logbook to keep track of the rents that were due, and Aris stepped in to oversee large repairs. He spent as much time as he could explaining things to me, but I had to figure out how to keep the books and handle most of the repairs. In this time before the internet, I used the yellow pages of the telephone book. My job was challenging.

But in the 1990s, time moved more slowly than it does now. People seldom moved out of their rent-controlled apartments. The residents had been neighbors for years. They knew each other and word soon spread that I tried hard to fix what was needed, which was different from the previous owners.

Aris called me twice a day. He came to visit me every day at four o'clock as my lover and protector. We often went out to dinner. He even found time to take me to the dentist and doctor. Occasionally, Aris sent his workers to the building to work on large repairs. His handymen also worked on his many other properties.

That's how I found out that Aris had another mistress. When one of his workmen told me that Aris went to her apartment too, I asked the worker for her telephone number. "What does she look like?" I wanted to know. The worker described her as a beautiful woman of Egyptian heritage named Laila, whom Aris had known and kept for many years before me. The floor fell from under me.

My heart in my mouth, I called her.

When Laila answered the phone, we began a conversation. She told me she knew about me also. She let me know that Aris's wife had known about her for many years.

"We are not the only ones, my dear, but the others are casual," Laila told me. She backed up her statements with facts of his whereabouts and I knew it was true. How much can one heart hurt?

This man, who made massive amounts of money, was politically important around the word, a married man whose wife and family adored him, found time for other women. Aris was my family too, my entire world. I loved him with my whole heart and soul. We had our afternoons, our dinners—where did he find time for another mistress? I was naïve.

I went back to my habit of using codeine number three and four pills, washing them down at night with Kahlua liquor, to try and keep the pain out of my heart. Finally, I got up the courage to confront Aris.

"No darling, it's not true, it's a joke," Aris said, telling me I was the only one. I did not believe him but I stayed with him. And, as many women do, I fell in love with him all over again.

∴

My relationships with the people in the building began to expand my horizons. Gerda Spiegler, my next-door neighbor, worked as a deputy for one of the five council people in the city of West Hollywood. After a few months of passing each other in the hallway and exchanging the customary greetings of "How are you?" she began inviting me into her apartment. We discovered a mutual liking and respect for each other.

"Come to a meeting of the West Hollywood Democratic Club with me," Gerda said one evening after dinner at her apartment. This led to many meetings and when the vacancy for Secretary became available, I was elected. I had a lot to learn about the many rules and regulations concerning how Democratic clubs are run and needed her help. After one particularly long meeting, I called her.

"What happened last night?" I asked her.

"Come over, I'll help you," Gerda offered.

I went to her apartment where she helped me write the minutes. I began to know her as the people of West Hollywood already did. She had been a leader in tenant rights and was one of the people who helped the city become incorporated.

Gerda had been spared from the Nazi concentration camps as a child, thanks to "Kindertransport," the operation to evacuate Jewish children from Nazi-controlled areas of Europe to the United Kingdom. When the war ended, Gerda returned to Austria and demanded that the government give her childhood house back. She was unsuccessful, but determined to try. Now, in the foyer of her apartment, Gerda kept an urn to remind her of her mother who had been exterminated, burned at one of the camps. Gerda was strong, so strong.

∷

"Please come in for a cup of coffee," said Suzette, a resident of whom I became very fond. A generation younger than me, Suzette was a beautiful woman of Irish and Lebanese descent. She had masses of shiny black hair, deep brown eyes, and her perfect white teeth gleamed when she laughed. We became good neighbors, then friends.

Managing the building gave me purpose, and Aris gave me financial and emotional stability, but my involvement with the people in the city of West Hollywood gave me confidence, pride in myself, and a strong sense of community. They made me feel that West Hollywood was my home.

But my life wasn't complete. I had a deep need that kept hitting me hard. I wanted to find my son. He would be in his late twenties by now. E.J. had always wanted to find him, and through the years she would longingly ask me, "Don't you want to know where he is?"

As any mother who has given a child up for adoption, I fantasized about my child. I spent years wondering: What was he like? Who did he look like? Who were his adoptive parents? What kind of an upbringing did they give him? What had he made of himself?

In 1993, a year after I moved into the apartment building, I asked Aris to help me find him.

"Are you certain you want to do this?" Aris asked.

"Yes," I replied.

Unusual for him, he asked again. "Are you sure?"

"Yes," came my firm reply.

Aris began dictating simple, persuasive letters to me, which I sent to Catholic Charities, the agency I had used for my son's adoption. I also wrote letters to every agency that searched for children given up for adoption.

∴∴

Meanwhile, I became more active in my political groups. I was elected to serve as the Vice President of the West Hollywood Democratic Club, and was an active member of Stonewall Democratic Club. Attending many club and city meetings, I saw how government works, and Aris and I had many conversations where he shared his valuable political insight.

As the Speaker of the House Tip O'Neill once said, "All politics is local." Our club was well respected and had great leadership. Local politicians sought our endorsement, many rising to higher office.

Below is a list of awards I received for my political work during this time.

2008 Named Democrat of the Year along with then-Mayor of San Francisco, Gavin Newsom, by the West Hollywood Democratic Club

2005 Stonewall Democratic Club, Los Angeles, Communications Vice President 2004 Named Democrat of the Year along with then-Los Angeles City Council Member Antonio Villaraigosa by the West Hollywood Democratic Club

2002 Received the Woman in Leadership Award from the West Hollywood Chamber of Commerce and the Women's Advisory Board

2000 Received the Rainbow Key Award from the City of West Hollywood and the West Hollywood Gay and Lesbian Advisory Board

1999 Received the Angeles Amidst Award from the City of West Hollywood for my work involving PATH

1998 Named Democrat of the Year 42nd Assembly District

1997 Received the Gerda Spiegler Member of the Year Award

1996 Served on the Los Angeles Council of Churches and received the Outstanding Volunteer Award

1994 Vice-President, Los Angeles Chapter, of "Neighbor To Neighbor," a statewide organization advocating for Universal Healthcare

∷

Even though I was busy with my political clubs, I had a desire to do more for my community. While sitting on my white couch in my apartment, I was very grateful for all that I had. I decided I wanted to do something good in the world.

One day, as I was reading the paper, an article about the West Hollywood Homeless Organization popped out. I thought, *I've almost been homeless myself. Helping the homeless is what I should do.* My next move was to make an appointment with Bob Erlenbusch, the president of the board.

When we met, I told him, "I want to be on the board."

"Well, you have to prove yourself first," he replied.

I began by creating a small library for the shelter. I asked my friends and neighbors to donate books, and transformed an empty room into a place for the residents of the shelter to use for reading or borrowing books. Then I worked with the staff on a Christmas party for the residents of the shelter. In the afternoons, I helped wherever I could. There was such great need. Bob saw my sincerity and, after the board's approval, I joined the board. Attending meetings, I tried to learn as much as I could.

∷

My life was full except for the nagging desire to know more about my son. Eventually, I received correspondence from Catholic Charities. They had sent me forms with many questions to complete, and called me on the telephone, assuring me they were looking into the matter. I was always waiting for their reply.

Finally, the day arrived in early 1995 when I received the letter from Catholic Charities telling me they had found my son. My heart was full of hope as they told me they had given him my telephone number.

Now the decision to contact me was up to him.

Aris Helping Me Work

Gerda and I

With Friends, Protesting

Having Fun with Friends

Receiving the Gerda Spiegler Award with Rob Reiner, David Cooley, Owner of the Abby, and Councilmember Antonio Villaraigosa

With Sal Guarriello, then Mayor of West Hollywood, at Red Carpet Academy Awards Party

Chapter Ten

MEETING MY SON

"Hello, Mother?"

The voice at the other end of the phone call was soft and shy. It belonged to my son.

"Yes. This is Julie," I said.

I was so thrilled to finally be connected to my son. "This is John, Mother." From then on, he called me Mother, as if he had never had one. He told me his name was John Laurence Trainer.

John told me that he was living in Fort Lauderdale, Florida. He had been in the Coast Guard, and was working to finish college with a major in political science. His adoptive father, Joe, was very supportive about John getting in touch with me. Joe lived near John and was divorced from John's adoptive mother.

A few weeks later, after several spontaneous telephone conversations, we made plans for me to fly to Florida so we could meet.

On the flight from Los Angeles, I couldn't contain my excitement.

"I'm going to meet my son for the first time since I gave him up for adoption," I told the stewardess. Happiness was shining on my face.

"Do you want me to take your picture with him when you get off the plane?" she asked.

"Yes, please," I said.

John was waiting for me at the gate. In the back of my mind I always had the question of who his biological father was. But when I saw him, I instantly knew.

When E.J. met with Catholic Charities to fill out the paperwork, I had given her two possible choices for who the baby's father might be. One was Bill Meade, the man who had introduced me to some of my wild times in Florida. The other was a casual friend who was tall and fair. E.J. intuitively made the right choice naming the father for the birth certificate. Tall, blond, and lean, he looked like his biological father, the casual friend.

On the tram ride from the airport to get his car, John looked at me like a hungry person, as if he wanted to devour me. Some of my first words to him were, "Thank God you are mentally okay." It was if I had a premonition and was subconsciously trying to make it so.

As we drove to where John lived, the conversation between us was like that of finding a new love, not the sexual kind but the family kind, wanting to know this human being we were so closely connected to. I wanted to know every minute of his life that had passed so far, but he had fewer questions.

John lived in the back end of an old wooden house surrounded by trees. It did not feel like anyone lived there. There were no pictures or personal items; it could have been anyone's house. We didn't stay long, but I had a chance to open the refrigerator door and saw it was stacked with Budweiser beer and nothing else. I thought this was strange.

John chose a nearby restaurant for our first dinner together and it was then he said, "I need a few more classes to graduate from college, Mother. I've been trying to hold down a job and study, but it's hard. I'm a news junkie which is why my degree will be in political science."

His service in the Coast Guard accounted for his excellent table manners. He told me he had been married once, with no children, and was now divorced. But he had glossed over his marriage, as if he did not want to tell me all the details. I stayed overnight in a nearby hotel and left the next day.

John and I talked on the phone every few days. We were getting to know each other. After a few months I flew again to Fort Lauderdale so we could spend three days together. John made reservations for me in a nearby hotel which was a chintzy, flowery place, very feminine with potpourri and fluffed-up pillows. The desk clerk told me that he had checked to make sure the room was perfect "for his mother."

John and I spent time in restaurants. We strolled along the marina near the boats and the water. We talked a lot, getting to know each other. I could see immediately the sweetness and kindness in him, along with a bit of desperation. He seemed to be searching to find himself.

Touring a local museum, John saw a Russian matryoshka doll set. He was proud of the fact that he had been to Russia.

"Let me buy this for you, Mother."

I happily accepted.

Once I went back to California, John and I talked often. He spoke with great love and respect about his adoptive father, Joe.

"My parents were divorced when I was a teenager," John let me know. He would not speak of his mother, Jean, almost as if he did not want to say anything about her, but the way he said she ate at fast food restaurants and watched a lot of TV, he seemed happy that she and I were opposites. I got the feeling that he thought I was the type of mother he always wanted. By contrast, John's face lit up when he spoke about his dad.

"He lives nearby, Mother. He really wants to meet you."

"Yes, John, let's make it the next trip."

"Do you want to know anything about your biological father?" I asked.

"No," he replied, and started talking about a baseball game he and Joe had seen together.

Within a few weeks I returned to meet the man who had raised my son. Dressed in a white casual pantsuit with John beside me, I walked up the steps to Joe's house to meet him. The woman Joe was living with excused herself, leaving the three of us to talk and become acquainted.

Joe played the guitar. After dinner we sat, sang songs, and talked for hours. I liked Joe immediately and immensely. He looked a lot like my brother Robert. This was a coincidence, but somehow it made everything better, as if we were a real family.

Joe did not want to speak of his ex-wife, Jean. Neither Joe nor John brought up John's older brother, Joe, Jr., who was Joe and Jean's biological child. But it was clear that Joe Sr. and John had as close a bond as any father and son, blood relation or not, could have. I thanked God.

∷

I sent John to Indiana to meet my brother Don, now divorced but still living in Indianapolis. Bonding over drinking beer and playing pool, they liked each other and felt the family connection. Through many phone calls with each other, Don was to remain a large part of John's life.

For Christmas of 1996, John and I went to Indianapolis so John could meet my brother Don's family. His ex-wife Maribeth and their two children, Aaron and his sister, were happy to meet the newest member of our famiily. Staying at Don's apartment along with us, Don's oldest son by his first marriage, Michael, completed the picture. I wanted John to meet everybody, and them to meet him. I was very proud of him.

∷

Robert and I had not seen each other since E.J.'s death in 1988, and there was little phone conversation between us. When I told him that I had found John, Robert and his wife, Sherry, told me their hands were full with their own two children. Robert told me they hoped to meet John sometime in the future.

∷

My life was enriched by my new relationship with my son. I also enjoyed working with my political and charity groups. The building continued to give me challenges and a secure job, and the friendships I began with my neighbors became deeper.

Gerda, my first real friend in the building, had not been feeling well. I began driving her to meetings and going with her to the doctor. On an afternoon like any other, she called me to her apartment and, in a very calm voice, said, "I have lung cancer."

"But you're strong, Gerda, you can beat this," I encouraged her.

She soon became very sick and I spent my days between her apartment and mine. At night I slept on a mattress on her living room floor, taking care of her and obeying her commands. The people she had worked with at the City called her The General. She deserved her nickname.

Eventually her doctor sent her to a hospice facility, a terrible place on Fairfax Avenue. Gerda told me she wanted to die at home. One afternoon, after she had spent a few days there, I picked her up, saying, "Come on, we're getting out of here," and took her home.

Through the next few months of home health care and visiting nurses, I seldom left her side. The afternoon that Gerda died, many of the City officials were in the living room. A terrible green bile gurgled up out of her mouth and all over her chest. She was gone.

In the Jewish religion, a mitzvah is loosely defined as doing a good deed with no thought of a reward. My mitzvah from Gerda was my complete acceptance into the West Hollywood community.

There were a lot of fun times in my community. I was invited to my friends' homes to watch them dress in drag for the Gay Pride Parade, sometimes riding in the parade myself.

But there were also sad times.

In 1999, I stood with my friends at the dedication of the Matthew Shepard Human Rights Triangle memorial in West Hollywood. His mother was there with all of us. In her speech, she said Matthew was just like everybody else. He was only different in whom he chose to love. And for this he was brutally murdered.

In this community I felt acceptance and love. I enjoyed working for equal rights for my friends. Standing on Santa Monica Boulevard with some friends, I heard people in passing cars yell "Faggot" or "You gay piece of trash." I felt the hatred hurled at us. Seeing this first-hand gave me a greater understanding.

Often, after a Stonewall meeting, young people would tell me stories of their coming out, the discrimination that came from their parents and families for being gay, and how much it hurt.

Although I was given many awards for my work, the one I most treasure is the "Rainbow Key," given by the Gay and Lesbian Advisory Board to me for standing up for the LGBT community and working on propositions against discrimination.

The fight for equality has come a long way. I am proud to have been part of that fight.

Aris heartily approved of my working for the good of my community. He also knew how happy I was to be in touch with John.

"I want to meet your son, darling," Aris told me. "Please find out when he can come to Los Angeles for a weekend. I will book him into a nearby hotel."

John arrived the following weekend. We both had lunch with Aris. The only comment Aris made to me later was, "John is a nice young man, but very weak."

For Aris to use "very" should have been a warning sign to me, but it wasn't.

That afternoon, a nasty storm had blown many leaves into the garage of the building. When we got home I put John to work sweeping them away, and discovered he was a good worker.

Saturday evening John and I arranged to have dinner with my friend Suzette. John seemed pleased to meet a friend of his mother. Arriving early, he and I walked the blocks of downtown Beverly Hills before dinner. We began a deep conversation.

"Why did you give me up for adoption, Mother?" John asked. "How could you? I don't understand." His voice was trembling.

I tried to explain that when he was born I could not take care of myself, let alone him. No matter how much I talked and tried to explain my circumstances, I could not make him understand. I did not tell him how my heart had broken or the desperate measure I took when I went to an attorney who put me into prostitution by promising he would get him back.

"Well, I was adopted to keep my mom and dad's marriage together. It didn't work and I am to blame," John said in a miserable tone of voice. "It's my fault they divorced. I feel like a failure."

We talked and talked, and I tried in vain to make him realize this was not so, and it was not his fault. I prayed that I got through to him.

The next day, he and I enjoyed ourselves at Sunday brunch at House of Blues on Sunset Boulevard. The people sitting next to us asked, "How are you related? We think you are, but can't figure it out."

John had lost his shyness by now, and he told them our story. They said, "Well, we knew because there is a glow coming from both of you."

After a wonderful weekend, John went home to Florida and I went back to working on my many projects.

Meeting John at the Airport

First Moments with John

Joe (John's adoptive father), John and Me

John and I in California

My Son, John

Chapter Eleven

PEOPLE ASSISTING THE HOMELESS, JOHN IN FLORIDA AND DENVER

My years of work with the West Hollywood Homeless Organization were fulfilling. It really made a difference in people's lives, which inspired me to spend as much time volunteering as I could. I worked my way up to become secretary of the board. In 1996, the office of the president became vacant. The board elected me to fill the position. I was thrilled because I was doing something productive.

"I will give you my advice," Aris said. He had encouraged me to take charge of my new office.

"For a non-profit to be successful, it needs to own its own building." His first recommendation made a lot of sense.

With the board's approval, Aris and I looked at many buildings that might be suitable to house the organization. We finally found a three-story, fifty-thousand-square-foot building at 340 North Madison Avenue in Los Angeles. It was gutted, filthy dirty, and had many problems. There was a load-bearing wall that was underground and not properly encased, and oil slicks on the floor. Aris, never one to back down from hard work, began the countless hours of negotiating a difficult escrow.

The original cost of the building was $2,600,000. Negotiating as only Aris could, the sale price became $800,000. I spent many hours lobbying the City of West Hollywood for a grant of $500,000. This, along with $250,000 from the CRA (California Redevelopment Agency) and $50,000 from Aris, and we had our price.

Aris and I went to see the surrounding neighbors of Madison Avenue, both residential and commercial, to convince them to accept a building to help the homeless in their neighborhood. Then we began the process of getting permits from the City of Los Angeles.

Aris also had the foresight to get the two adjacent lots, located at 333 and 337 North Westmoreland Avenue, at a cost of $150,000.

Escrow closed in June 1998. We had a building! And two adjacent lots. But we had a building that needed approximately seven million dollars of rehabilitation work. And we had no money.

∴∴

With board permission, Aris and I went to see Joel John Roberts, the CEO of People Assisting the Homeless (PATH), located on Cotner Avenue in West Los Angeles. Founded by Claire West Orr and her husband, Rev. Charles Orr, it provided many needed services to the homeless, including transitional housing. After countless long board meetings of both the West Hollywood Homeless Organization and PATH, we merged, keeping the name of PATH.

Our new board of approximately fifteen people, and of which I became a regular member, was a volunteer board and we received no compensation for our time, giving our services freely. Even though it was a very serious business, our board was like a sitcom that had the cast and characters to make a hit show, and our meetings were productive and enjoyable.

With Claire at the helm, we dove in and began the task of raising the seven million dollars needed to make the Madison Avenue building ready to serve homeless people. No small task for a non-profit. Along with a great many unsung volunteers and staff, the board jumped into organizing house parties, capital campaign letters, mailers, and fundraising events.

Using my political connections from serving as vice-president of the West Hollywood Democratic Club, and Aris using his weighty political and financial connections, we went to see politicians, telling them of the Madison Avenue building. We asked for, and received, help and guidance for grants and other avenues of government funding.

After many architectural meetings, proposals, inspections, asbestos removal, environmental reports, and decisions about the functional design of the building, we had our grand opening on April 11, 2002.

Becoming the cornerstone for PATH's phenomenal growth, the building design was an innovation, unlike any other homeless service agency. It was a one-stop shop, a brand-new idea for serving the homeless.

Every board member worked very hard, especially those who served as president. But Claire West Orr, at the top of her game in fundraising and bringing in large donations, and Joel John Roberts, who committed himself to ending homelessness, stand out.

It had taken six years to open the doors at 340 N. Madison. Even though I had worked myself into a sickly state, this was one of the happiest periods of my life. I knew it was the best thing I had ever done, saying, "Thank you God, for choosing me to help with this."

I am very thankful to everyone who made this happen, and I am so proud of my continued involvement with PATH. When someone asked me how I did what I did, I answered, "Nobody told me I couldn't." A simple statement, but very true.

PATH grew to become one of the leading non-profit organizations in California to combat homelessness. We focus on moving people off the streets, through the shelter system, and into their own permanent home by providing the full continuum of services from streets to home. We have programs in about 150 cities, assisting roughly 20% of the homeless population in California.

"I want to be a force for good, and change the world," Aris once told me. Well, Aris, you did.

∷

Throughout this busy time, I stayed in touch with my son by phone. On one of our calls, John had shared some information about his living situation.

"I'm working part–time wherever I can find a job, Mother, and I have one year left to complete college."

Knowing how badly he wanted to graduate, I called the college and made appointments for John and myself to meet with the faculty. The next month, we went to the campus to meet and talk with his instructors, setting his curriculum for the next year. It pleased me that he was majoring in political science, as I thought he and Aris would have common ground for a relationship.

"My car needs fixing, Mother. I have a place to take it. And I'm going to move in with a friend, to cut down on expenses."

I gave him a check to pay for school, car, and living expenses, thinking he was on his way. Over the course of the next few months we talked on the phone often. When I asked him how he was doing, he told me of a paper due, what grade he received on the last paper, and experiences in class or on campus. I was filled with bliss, until the bubble popped when I caught him in a lie. Then another.

I was walking across the blue carpet in my apartment, phone in hand, when John told me he had taken the money I gave him and blown it.

"I never attended a class either, Mother. My car still needs repairs and I am not getting along with my roommate."

His revelations shocked me. My heart went out of my body. I felt like I was losing him for the second time, knowing he had huge problems.

I immediately called his father, Joe.

"I am so thankful you know what's been happening with John. Now we can talk about this." The relief was evident in Joe's voice. "I haven't known who I could talk to about his problems."

Joe loved John unconditionally. He told me he had become troubled by John's behavior when he was thirteen.

He began with the story of John riding a freight elevator by himself to the top. On the way up, he let out loud, blood-curdling screams as Joe waited below. On the trip down, the screaming stopped. When he stepped off the elevator to greet Joe, his face was completely bland. Joe told me this story many times as if he was trying to figure out what made him do this.

"He never seems to eat," Joe said. "He drinks beer night and day and smokes cigarettes all the time. I don't know what is to become of his future," Joe said in a worried voice.

Then Joe told me when John was seventeen, he took his car into a field behind their house and tried to kill himself by asphyxiation. Joe looked out a window of the house, saw him in the car and realized what he was doing.

"Stop, stop, John!" Joe said as he ran into the field, waving his arms and screaming. He got to John in time to prevent serious injury. Joe knew John was off balance but matter-of-factly accepted the situation.

Joe would end our calls by saying, "You are his mother. Maybe you can figure him out."

These should have been warning signs to me, but I was still on the high of finding the child I had so long ago given up for adoption.

∷

"Please, John, get a physical and get your thyroid checked," I implored him. I have thyroid problems so I thought he might, too. "And please, try not to smoke so much."

I did not know what else to do. I had been a heavy smoker, too. I found it hard to quit and only did so because Aris really hated the smell of cigarette smoke. But it wasn't easy for me. I tried to quit seven times and could not. Finally getting down on my hands and knees and begging God to help me, I quit.

∷

"Let me send you pictures from my childhood, Mother," John said one day.

I received the pictures, looking at them hungrily. As I put them into an album, I saw that he and I looked exactly alike when we were babies. It gave me comfort that the pictures of John's early childhood looked like any American family of the time.

"I'm moving to Denver, Mother," John said, on a phone call to me a few months later. "I'm going to work in the food service business."

People always liked John, and he made good friends, moving in with one of them. Again, I hoped he was on his way to a stable life.

He never hesitated to pick up the phone and say, "I need to see you, Mother."

When he said that, I dropped everything and went to see him. I made several trips to Denver, staying in a hotel. I got to see the restaurant where he worked and met his friends.

We planned a trip for the next Thanksgiving. When he picked me up from the airport, John began driving his car erratically. I was unnerved when he drove with his fists gripping the steering wheel and his teeth clenched. He was speaking to me, but whatever he was saying was gibberish and made no sense. My hair went up on the back of my neck and chills ran up and down my arms and legs.

"My God, John wants to kill me," I thought to myself. We continued our trip to his friend's house for Thanksgiving. The dinner was good, but there was a lot of drinking among the six or so people there. I said I didn't feel well, then I booked a flight home the next day.

∷

Back in Los Angeles, I still didn't recognize the significance of his unpredictable behavior. We continued to speak on the phone often over the next few months and I invited him to a family gathering at my brother Robert's cabin in Idaho. Robert and his wife Sherry invited Don and his children Michael, Aaron, and Aaron's sister. This meant John would get to see his blood family together for the first time.

I was anxious to meet Robert and Sherry's two children, now in their teens. In the past they had told me their life was too full and harried for me to visit, though I suspect some of those years they were afraid of having an ex-con in their house. But now our days in Utah were spent river rafting or swimming in cold water streams. At night we played board games and looked at the sky.

The two weeks went by fast, but John was in a major downswing. I wondered if this was because he felt the lack of family growing up, but there were bigger problems. After our vacation, John and I promised to talk often by phone. He returned to Denver and I went back to Los Angeles.

Once I got home, I had an attraction to another married man even though I was still very much in love with Aris. This conflict made me realize I was not emotionally balanced.

Ruth Williams, a friend from the West Hollywood Democratic Club, referred me to a psychologist, Dr. Stephanie Royal. Our weekly sessions helped me understand how I look at the world. She also made me take a good look at myself. With her help, I realized I had come out swinging after I was raped as a teenager. I saw the world in a combative way, and needed to soften my ways.

E.J. had been the most important person in my life. I was defensive when Dr. Royal tried to blame some of my emotional problems on her. I got mad when she was critical of E.J. I knew that my mother had done her best with everything that life had dealt her. It took a while for me to realize that E.J. had been responsible for much more negativity in my life than Daddy. I started to gain many valuable insights into myself.

I began to realize the depth of pain and self-destruction I had caused myself, and the pain I had caused my family. I knew I had been one big ball of pain and had to hurt myself and everyone around me to be able to hit bottom. Physical and emotional rock bottom.

I started to work on myself. It is called work because it is not fun to look at our own destructive behavior. But we need to look to find out what made us act and react in certain ways.

How did I begin to try and forgive myself for all my crimes I had committed against others? I lay awake at night thinking about how I had hurt people, financially and emotionally, and betraying myself. I could not trust myself, a horrifying revelation.

Shame and agony came to me as I realized what I had done. Too many years had passed for me to find the companies to whom I wrote bad checks, and some of my crimes were not only writing bad checks, but acts I had not been arrested for. I was afraid to go to these people and say, "Forgive me," because I was afraid of being arrested.

Silently telling them I was sorry, I asked many times for their forgiveness. Each day became a test of character, to do the right thing. It was really so simple: just get up and do the right thing. A revelation.

This led to a firmer foundation and gradually my trust in myself began rebuilding. Realizing that parts of me are good, I started to treat myself better, and then I treated others better.

"Come to see me when you are unhappy, or if you feel your life is not working," the therapist said, as our visits lessened.

When Dr. Royal moved to Florida, we took long breaks from her treatment, some lasting many months at a time. She had me read many books, among which were *Adult Children of Alcoholics* by Janet Geringer Woititz, Ed.D. and *What You Think of Me Is None of My Business* by Terry Cole-Whittaker, which helped me learn about letting go of some of my negative thoughts and behavior.

Dr. Royal taught me the importance of getting professional help in times of mental need. She had a great impact on my life.

PATH, People Assisting the Homeless
I Was Named PATH 25 Year Honoree in 2010

Chapter Twelve

THE FINAL MISTRESS YEARS, JOHN IN TEXAS

The world was Aris's oyster, and he knew it. He walked like a man who had made millions of dollars and his eyes twinkled as if he knew the universe always had a present for him. But when his wife of twenty years passed away in 2001, the lights dimmed in Aris's eyes and he lost some of the swagger in his step.

He immediately made plans for us to go to Europe on a whirlwind trip for two months. I gave my tenants the telephone number for Aris's office to call when they needed repairs, then pre-paid the bills, and sent a memo asking tenants to put their rent checks under my door, to be deposited when I returned.

"Pack only two small suitcases that you can carry with you," Aris told me before we left. Then he had me look at cars. "Pick out the Volvo you want, darling, and when we return to the States it will be yours," he said. Volvo had a promotion that, at no charge, allowed you to buy a car in the States, pick it up in Sweden and drive it around Europe for months before Volvo shipped it back to the U.S.

We were off. Flying to Sweden to pick up the car, we took a ferry that transported both us and the car to Germany.

Driving on an autobahn in Germany with a man who was now in his seventies was an experience in itself. There are rarely speed limits on these highways so most drivers go upwards of ninety miles an hour. The few times I drove the car, I knew it was either drive or die. We arrived safely in Hamburg to meet Aris's sister, Georgette.

Georgette and I liked each other immediately from the first formal "How do you do?" We became more relaxed in conversation as we got to know each other. But most of the time she and Aris spoke in German or Greek, as English was less comfortable for Georgette.

The three of us then went to an island off the eastern coast of Germany, where we spent a week in a lovely hotel, with frequent trips for sightseeing.

Switzerland was next as we drove through the beautiful countryside to get to Lausanne. Aris's other sister, Ellie, who was quite ill, was living in a grand building that was half hospital and half hotel. Swans swam on the lake surrounding the building, visible to all.

After a few days we continued to Italy, where we stopped in a small town named Parma. I awoke in the morning and sleepily said to Aris, "Who are you and where are we?"

That summed up how tired I was.

Athens, the next stop, was Aris's birthplace. The Acropolis and other famous places followed, but they were lost on me. When Aris pointed out the condo in Athens that he and his deceased wife had enjoyed, it felt as though he was reliving his trips with her, even though I was the one present.

Perhaps this was how he tried to handle his grief, but it did not make me feel good. It did not matter to me where we went or what we saw, I was starting to feel miserable. When I met friends of Aris's, I was largely ignored. It was too soon after the death of his wife, plus women were not important when men were present.

∷

There were some lighter moments during our stay at one of the best hotels in Athens.

"This is room 207, and we are going to the beach now," Aris said on the telephone to the concierge. An employee of the hotel met us at the beachside door, carrying a beach umbrella and towels. Walking with us until we reached the beach, the employee set up the umbrella and placed the towels over our chairs. Both of us were good swimmers and Aris and I swam in the ocean each day until time to nap before dinner.

When we were driving, through the car window I saw a gypsy standing on a hill holding a baby in her arms. I looked at her black hair and dark eyes and wondered what she felt as she looked back at me. Even though our worlds were light years apart, I felt a bond, a deep connection with her. Looking at donkeys on countryside around the city, I was taken to another time, a more peaceful time of days past.

It had been prearranged for Aris's son and daughter, their spouses and four children, along with Aris's attorney and his wife, to meet us in Athens. When they arrived, Aris rented a small yacht, complete with captain, a cook, the cook's wife, and another crew member. As we began island-hopping around the Aegean Sea, swimming and eating, the mood became lighter.

After three weeks, we said goodbye to the family, then drove to Basel, Switzerland, to put the car on a train, destination Hamburg. Aris and I slept in the sleeper car. The next morning, the train arrived in Hamburg, where we stopped for a last goodbye with Georgette. She and her housekeeper served tea as only one who grew up with her own governess could do. It is a way of life I am glad I saw.

Amsterdam was next. We walked the famous sidewalks and enjoyed gondola rides on the canals, and, after spending a few nights, left the car to be shipped to me in the States.

As we stood on the cement shipping dock, Aris surprised me when he asked, "Will you marry me, darling?"

After two months of traveling, I was so tired that all I said was, "I want to go home." It did not help that I had been "chipping," which is taking small bites of pills, uppers and downers.

We flew home to Los Angeles. Although I ate constantly during our vacation, I lost eleven pounds. Thoroughly exhausted, I returned to my apartment and slept for three or four days.

Aris's insurance company called me to ask me if I had received the car yet. They told me that Aris had put the car and the insurance in the name of "Julie Anagnos." Aris assumed that we would be married shortly.

∷

My love was a very wealthy, good-looking bachelor. Women had thrown themselves at him before, but now it was out in the open. He was a natural womanizer who loved attention, found almost all women beautiful, and lit up in their presence.

I suspect he had a hard time saying no to any woman who approached him, but my revelation about him came at a political event that I attended without him. I was seated next to a beautiful woman whom I did not know. Someone asked her who she was dating. Without skipping a beat, she said, "Aris Anagnos." I never had a hint of this relationship. It was too much for me.

Aris continued to ask me to marry him. I knew he loved me, but out of love and a desire to keep me safe, he wanted to control me. I did not want to be a bird in a golden cage.

One night, he came to my front door. As he stepped in, he opened his arms and said, "I love you, darling. Please stop all this nonsense and marry me."

"No," I said emphatically. "Now please leave."

His eyes burned like black coals staring out at me. I felt the depth of our relationship.

Now I spent most of my time alone. I would awaken at four o'clock every morning, sob heavily, then go back to sleep. The pain from not seeing him was tremendous. And I had huge crying jags during the day, feeling sorry for myself. I wondered how I, an old woman in her fifties living in Los Angeles, would ever find my lover, my husband.

On visits to my therapist, Dr. Royal asked me what I did after my crying jags.

"I just keep on going."

She knew I would be okay.

This was the end of the romantic part of the relationship between Aris and me. But we continued our relationship of love and caring, talking often and seeing each other occasionally for dinner.

While Aris and I were in Europe, I'd kept in touch with John. John knew how I was feeling from my first "hello" on the phone, so when he called and I discussed my feelings about Aris, he said, "Oh, Mother, please don't marry that man." I thought he had a much higher opinion of Aris, but he reassured me that I had made the right choice.

Sometime later, John told me that he had worked himself up the ladder in the Denver restaurant business. He sounded very proud, saying, "Mother, I got a promotion to sous-chef, but it means I would have to relocate to a small town in Texas."

I was concerned because I knew John relied heavily on his close friends. This would mean making all new friends. My mother's intuition told me that this might be difficult.

John had not been in Texas long when the apartment manager of his complex called me.

"John threw himself out of a three-story window. He's in bed in his apartment, alone."

He had been taken to a local hospital by ambulance. After a short stay, he was released with only a broken coccyx. I flew to Texas immediately, renting a car and a hotel room near his apartment.

When I arrived, John was flat on his back in bed. The first thing I noticed was how neat his apartment was and that the only pictures displayed were of Joe, his father, and myself. I was deeply touched.

"How do you feel, John? Let me look at you and make sure there are no broken bones, and that you can move everything." Again, there was only beer in his refrigerator, so I went to the grocery store and bought TV dinners, eggs and bread and juice. I came back, we ate, then John slept.

When I got back to my motel room I was feeling very nervous. I spent hours picking at my face with a nail file, making my face deep red all over. Then I took pills to sleep.

The next morning, I went back to John's apartment. I tried to assess him and his situation.

"Mother, I went to the furthest part of the apartment, ran full speed, and crashed through the plate glass window, three stories below," he told me. "I don't know why."

Tree branches broke his fall. He landed on the cement, right on his butt.

"My last thought was of your mother, my grandmother, and I saw her face on the way down," he told me. I knew John was in serious trouble. But seeing him alive, in front of me, I concentrated on getting him well.

I called Aris to ask him what to do.

"Get him to a psychiatrist," he replied quickly.

Sitting on the floor beside John's bed, we went through the yellow pages of the phone book together to find one. We picked a name. I called and the doctor said to bring him in.

∷

John's apartment was on the third floor. Because his appointment was not a medical emergency, I could not call a regular ambulance. Going through the yellow pages again, we found a private ambulance service. They came up to the apartment, then strapped John onto a flat board of plywood and carried him down three flights of stairs.

"Hold on, John, hold on," I told him. I could see he was in intense pain.

I rode in the ambulance with him. He was carried into the psychiatrist's office, which I had made sure was on the first floor. There we were, John strapped onto the plywood plank on the floor, me with my bright red picked face, and the kind doctor, sitting in his chair facing us.

The doctor had John's blood drawn, then asked John questions about every area of his life. He and John talked for many hours.

Finally, he looked at us and said, "John, you are bipolar."

John and I looked at each other,

What was bipolar? I didn't know and neither did John. It was 2002 and the disorder had not been widely publicized.

John and I learned. We looked it up and discussed it.

I tried to put a happy face on the disease by saying that a lot of bipolar people were brilliant and talented. I will never forget John's hollow tone of voice when he looked at me and said, "Mother, all I want is to be normal."

∷

I stayed in Texas to care for him. He used crutches and a round pillow to sit on, easing the pain on his coccyx. In my rented car, I got him to the doctor and picked up his medications.

Slowly he started getting better. I watched his progress every day as his body and muscles mended.

Once, when he came out of the shower with a towel around him, I looked at the shape of his bones and the way he was built. He had my body. It seemed impossible to me, but there it was, on his body. Exactly, right down to the shape of his feet.

Remembering John's service in the Coast Guard, I found a Veterans Administration hospital that was close by. It was an excellent resource, providing good mental and physical facilities. We made several trips to the hospital, getting him enrolled and providing a future resource for him. John was also learning to take care of himself in other ways.

I showed him how to keep a checking account, how to file his important papers, and other basics of life. When he started cooking small meals, I knew he would be okay, and I returned to Los Angeles. It had been an intense three weeks.

During this time Aris had taken ill, and was diagnosed with large cell arteritis, a disease of the circulatory system causing painful swelling in the blood vessels all through the body. When I got to his house, he was lying in bed. He was ill and full of grief for his former wife. I looked at this man who was suffering.

"Do you want to live or do you want to die? If you want to live, get up and get walking," I said, making him do his own laundry, which meant a long walk from the bedroom to the laundry room.

Aris had night sweats from his disease. Getting up in the middle of the night to help him change his sweat-drenched t-shirt, I took two ten-milligram Ambien to go back to sleep. Even through the Ambien I could feel his deceased wife's presence in the room, strongly looming over the foot of the bed where we slept, where they used to sleep. It gave me the heebie-jeebies.

Purry, the cat, jumped from dresser to bedpost as if he too could feel her presence. It did not help that Georgette told me Aris had taken the ashes of his deceased wife, and spread them in a circle around the house.

I knew Aris needed me with him. I stayed a couple of months, leaving to manage the apartment building when necessary.

While at Aris's house, I read books on bipolar disorder, trying to figure out how to help John. His body, young and healthy, had made a rapid recovery. I read that bipolar disorder is a condition that causes severe mood swings. People who have it suffer from deep depression a lot of the time, while also having manic moods where they feel euphoric. Sadly, most of the time their feelings are depressed, which causes them to self-medicate with drugs or alcohol. Doctors often prescribe anti-depressants that must be taken all the time.

"I promise you I am taking my meds, Mother," he said.

He made plans to move back to Denver to be near his friends and get another job in the restaurant business. But I could hear wide mood swings in his voice when we talked. I would question him to learn more about how he was feeling.

"I don't like how I feel when I take my meds, Mother. They make me feel slow and dull," he said.

I went into despair, knowing I was really losing him.

What could I do? I thought about flying to Denver to make him take his pills every day, but this was not practical. Knowing how much he loved me, I told him if he took his meds he would live; if not, he would die. But I still didn't understand the extent of his mental illness.

∴

After a few months John called, deep sorrow showing in his voice. "Mother, Dad died."

"Oh, no! What happened?" I asked.

"He had a heart attack."

"Do you want me to meet you in Denver?" I asked John.

"No, Mother. I want to go to the mountains to be alone."

Aris and I at Beach

Aris and I at Sea

Me in Sweden

Aris in Sweden

Aris and I at Farm in Germany

Aris and I at the Acropolis in Athens

Chapter Thirteen

JOHN, MY SON JOHN

I continued to offer to go to Denver to be with John or to arrange for him to come to Los Angeles to stay with me.

"I found another job, Mother. It's with my friends in the restaurant business. I don't need to see you right now," he said on one of our conversations.

He sent me cards and one letter. In the letter he told me he was grateful I had found him, and said:

"You are my Mother and I am your blood. You are the most important thing in my life, for without you I would not have a life. Our relationship is ours, we understand each other and somehow instinctively know when the other is in need. For me, I cannot imagine a greater gift."

I loved my son, but I did not realize how much he needed me. I knew that too many years had passed before I found him. I had not been able to raise him. The love we shared now may have come too late to be effective in his life.

I was angry. Angry at John because, deep down, I knew he was not taking his meds. Angry at myself because I did not know what to do. I knew the anger came out of self-preservation that came from the early betrayal in my life. During therapy I learned I always got angry at the people I loved most. Now, I was trying to effectively handle that anger.

∵∵

My relationship with Aris had continued on a friendship level. One day in 2003, I got a memorable phone call from him.

"Hello and goodbye," Aris said briskly. "I'm getting married again."

He told me about his new wife. They were leaving for Greece soon.

So that was that. I continued my work at the apartment building, which was easier for me now. I had great support from my handyman, Alex, who handled all the repairs for my residents.

In June 2007, I turned sixty years old. In August, John would turn forty-one. On Mother's Day that year, he called me and left a message on my answering machine, saying, "I know our relationship did not turn out as either one of us wanted it to, but I want you to know that I will always love you."

In July, I worked to get the swimming pool at the apartment building ready for summer. I spent time with the workmen who had come to repair and re-plaster the bottom of the pool. The process fascinated me, and I learned how the blue of the sky reflected off the white pool plaster, making the walls of the pool look blue. The work took longer than expected but at the end of the day the plastering was finished. The workers started to fill the pool with water, telling me they had to leave.

"You have to keep filling the pool or it will leave a mark on the sides. The process will take six or seven hours to finish. You can't turn off the water until the pool is full, or it will leave a permanent line."

They stressed the importance of this. I understood their concern and promised that I wouldn't touch the water valve until the water reached the proper level.

It was July 11. I was alone in my apartment that summer night when I received a call.

"Is this Julie Summers?" a man with a brusque voice asked me.

"Yes," I said.

"Are you John Trainer's mother?"

"Yes," I replied. The thought went through my mind that John had been arrested for something.

"This is the county morgue in Denver, Colorado. We have your son here. He committed suicide."

My body went into pure shock. Somehow I had the presence of mind to ask the man for his name and telephone number, telling him I would call him back. He gave them to me, along with the name and telephone number of the apartment manager for the building where John lived.

Then my mind split from my body, my heart broke into pieces, and died.

I sat in my chair for many hours, then I walked out onto the patio. It was dark, and the lights of the pool showed it being filled with water. I could hear the rushing sound of water, but that was all that was real to me.

In a daze, I called my friend in the building.

"Suzette, please, will you come to my apartment?"

I wanted to tell someone what had happened. In my shock, all I could think about was the water running into the pool. I asked her to walk down the stairs with me to check on the water level. My body felt as if it had no bones in it.

"My son John killed himself," I said in a matter-of-fact voice, so as not to alarm her. She could see I was visibly shaken.

Suzette took my arm to steady me. We walked down the stairs to the pool. I showed her where to find the shut-off valve.

"Please turn off the water when the pool is filled," I asked her. My feet didn't touch the ground as we walked back to my apartment. I could not feel my body. I was elevating, but this time I knew it.

Once I got back into my apartment, I took two Ambien, thinking I could put off the pain by sleeping. It did not work. I couldn't sleep. I lay on my white couch, looking up at the popcorn ceiling, then down at the cherry wood floor.

I could feel John's spirit and kept saying to him, "Keep walking, keep walking, keep walking, John."

I felt his soul was in danger, and it became a mantra. "Keep walking, John, keep walking." I said it out loud all night long, never sleeping, as if I could save John's soul by doing this.

The next morning, I called John's apartment manager.

"John had been very depressed, and did not leave his apartment for many days," he told me. "His cat, a black cat, meowed and meowed for a long time. Then yesterday John took a twelve-gauge shotgun, put it between his toes and blew his head off."

I thought, John has never seen a gun, let alone owned one.

Like some people in shock who have to keep talking and talking, the manager got very detailed.

"His body was blown to bits, splattered all over. There's a suicide note. Do you want me to read it to you?"

"No," I replied. I knew that if I heard what John had written I would go someplace in my mind and never come back. My mind was splintering, cracking.

The manager told me how sorry he was, how much he liked John. He told me he would take care of the cat and anything else I needed to have done.

∷

When I hung up, I tried to compose myself to make a difficult phone call. I called Jean Trainer, the woman who had raised John. I had called her just once before, soon after locating my son. Then, she had told me John had been raised in a small town in Florida, saying, "John was a delightful child. He ran all over the neighborhood asking people if he could help them."

She sounded as if she truly loved him.

To call her now, with the news of John's suicide, was instinctual. She was his legal mother. I knew that calling her would cut all my legal ties to John. But I had to call her; it would not be right if I didn't. After our call, she kept me out of everything, including her decision for John's burial. It was as if she still wanted him all to herself.

The next morning the phone rang. It was my brother Don's wife, Maribeth. Over the years I had spent a lot of time with Don and his family in Indiana. Don and Maribeth had a beautiful daughter and a wonderful son named Aaron, whom I adored. This little boy and I connected the first time we met, when he was a baby. I loved watching him grow up. I used to say that John was my soul, but Aaron was my heart.

Maribeth and Don had divorced, but Maribeth and I stayed in close contact. She started talking in a voice as unreal as mine.

"Aaron had emergency surgery on his throat. After his tracheostomy he will have to have a permanent trach in his neck. They found cancer."

Aaron, who was twenty now and had sung around the world in a well-known choir, was going to lose his voice. More importantly, his future health prognosis was unknown. This was horrifying news to me, a one-two punch to the gut.

I did not tell Maribeth about John. I could not handle the reality of it.

It was impossible for me to handle anything. There was so much grief that I couldn't take it all in. I remained in massive shock. I didn't have the clarity to do simple things.

I waited a week, until after Don's birthday, to call and tell him.

"Noooo," Don said, with heartbreak in his voice.

He had loved John. They'd had a good uncle-nephew relationship, just the two of them, and stayed in touch with many phone calls. I did not call anyone else. I told no one in the building except Suzette. I asked her to drive me to my meetings.

∷

"I am stepping down from my vice-presidency," I told my fellow board members at the next meeting of the West Hollywood Democratic Club. "My son killed himself." I could barely get the words out of my mouth.

The other members accepted my resignation. They showed me respect and sympathy. We were a community that had been through many years of losing people to AIDS. Some of the people in our group had knowledge of what bipolar meant.

After withdrawing from the West Hollywood Democratic Club, I knew I had to do the same with my position at PATH.

"I need to take a leave of absence," I stated at the next board meeting, telling them why. My fellow board members showed great concern.

My energy was frenetic and I desperately needed an outlet. I spent the next few months with my handyman, Alex, changing pipes under sinks and the flex hoses going from toilet to wall. There were seventy-six sinks and forty-eight toilets in the building. We changed every one of them. I knew I had to keep busy or I would go crazy, stark raving mad.

∷

Unknowingly, I had set the stage to grieve. I did not have to answer to anyone, and I was alone to grieve. I went to bed.

Waking up, it felt as if a big, fat child were sitting on me, pushing the life out of me, trying to squeeze me into a pancake.

The pain had tentacles and they would grab my back, squeezing me. My back and chest were locked in a painful, vise-like grip. "Breathe, breathe," I told myself. I couldn't breathe, and hoped I would get very small and disappear.

I am going to have a heart attack, I thought.

"Take my heart out of my body, please God." I prayed. "If not, then I will forget my body because this is too much to bear."

My heart feels like it is getting bigger. It is too big for my body. Surely it must explode. Big tears fall, just fall out, slowly and constantly. I don't blink very often, there is no need. I can't let anything in.

I wake up again and again and again. There is no night, no day. The building is very quiet, as if everyone knows.

I see John in the doorway of my bedroom, leaning against the doorjamb, smoking a cigarette like always. He is wearing a long-sleeved, blue-checkered shirt and watching over me. I think to myself, why oh why didn't I take the time to shop to get him a shirt? Did I ever tell him how nice he always looked? I don't think so. I cry very hard after that, very hard.

I drift off to sleep, then awaken to ask, "Am I still here? Where is here?" I wake up to find John still standing in the bedroom doorway, guarding me, then I drift off to sleep again.

My heart hurts so bad. I do not have to do anything, nothing is important. Any glimmer of reality is pain. Am I still alive? I touch my body, yes, it is mine. I must shower, that is a good goal. But hygiene doesn't matter. I can't move, it is impossible to move. I don't need to take Ambien, it seems I am disconnected from my conscious mind. I go back to sleep.

I must have eaten and drunk water. In a dreamlike state, I stood in the kitchen, making toast and peanut butter. Then I went back to bed. I had no concept of time. I knew I was doing things correctly, just very slowly, things I'd done a million times and had the routine of habit down. What did it matter if I did these things?

But I must eat. Everyone knows that. And so I try to move. I'm having my second nervous breakdown.

I try to get up and go to the couch in the living room, but it seems like it is a long way. I have no body, and I almost lose consciousness and fall. The clothes hamper catches me. I roll on it to get back into bed.

Later I realized my blood pressure was extremely low, and had taken large drops.

⁘

Eventually, one day I make it to the couch and look out at the world. Nothing is real, there is no sound. That's it, there is no sound. I am in a bubble; no everyone else is in a bubble and I am just a ball of pain. I don't blink. Is this what insanity feels like? Close, very close.

I hear the backup beeping from a truck or the sounds of a fire engine. But that is not my reality. Life goes on without me. Everything sounds different. I fade in and out.

I hear the birds chirping. It is a good sign, life-affirming. I look out, but my eyes only let so much in. Eventually I know I am breathing. I feel like there has been a circle of angels around me, trying to keep out the pain.

Finally, I went to a Japanese grocery store. The only thing I ate for the next six months was raw fish eggs and candy. When I left my apartment, I wanted to put a sign on my forehead saying: "Be Kind To Me — My Son Just Committed Suicide." I wondered how many people we meet each day also want to put a sign on their forehead describing the pain in their heart.

I thought of starting a business like this, only maybe with wristbands, which were just coming into vogue. This was a very good sign that I was getting back to myself. I was here. The pain was very, very heavy, but I was here.

⁘

During this time the apartment building had been eerily quiet.

Now, tenants began leaving messages on my answering machine. "This is Amy. My dishwasher is broken."

I wrote it down, then called my handyman. When Alex came to my apartment, I slid my arm around the partially opened door, making sure he couldn't see me.

"Amy's dishwasher needs to be fixed," I said, and dropped Amy's apartment keys into his hand. When he returned after fixing it, I slid my arm around the door and felt the keys drop into my hand.

Each month as always, the residents left their rent checks under my door. I wrote the payments down in my rent book. Alex gave me my mail once a week. I wrote checks for the bills. Once a month Alex went to the bank and mailed the checks.

One day I got a phone call from John's brother, Joe Jr.

"May I have John's social security number?" he asked me. "And do you know of any bank accounts that were John's?"

Then he asked if I had knowledge of any of John's credit cards. Reasonable questions, but he sounded as if he was up to something.

"Does your mother know you are calling?" I asked him.

Click went the phone.

∷

Aris called. "Are you all right, darling?"

"Yes," I replied. "Please leave me alone."

Aris had started divorce proceedings from his new wife. He called me many times, ignoring my request.

I started to tell people, people that I casually knew. A few of the people I told reacted as if the pain of suicide was a disease. They did not want to get too close to me for fear of catching it.

After a few months my yoga teacher called.

"Julie, this is Lauri," she said, leaving a message on my machine. "I haven't seen you in a long time and I'd like to come over."

I returned her phone call, and invited her to visit me. Before she arrived, I took a shower. I couldn't remember the last time I had taken one.

Lauri met me at the front door. We sat together for a while. She asked if I would like her to visit occasionally so I could get back into my routine of taking yoga.

I let Lauri in once a week. She pushed my body to move, very gently at first. My intuitive self was becoming clearer, and I knew things about her and people surrounding her without being told by her. She said I was psychic. I said I definitely was not, but this was the beginning of my deep intuition for myself.

"I want you to meet David," she announced one day. "He is a spiritual man who is well known for his breathing practice. It helps those in emotional need."

I started seeing him once a week, very carefully making the drive to his house, then lying on his worktable and doing the deep breathing exercises he taught me. I gradually started coming back to life. This breathing linked me deeper into the spiritual world, and centered me in this one. To me, David is a miracle worker.

Lauri also introduced me to Yi Chen, a masseuse in Santa Monica. Her hands did not seem to touch my body, but I felt the effects of her massage for many days.

"I can see the pain in my clients by the color of the aura that surrounds the pain," she told me. "I see a lotus flower in your stomach," she told me. "It is a healing omen and very rare," she said.

∷

Lauri, David, and Yi Chen were the only people I saw during the period following John's death and into 2008. They brought me back to reality, a different reality from before. This one included all the planes of my prior reality, but had many dimensions. John's death had broken my heart wide open, so that I could feel other people's suffering, their energy, and the spirit that is in their hearts.

John and Aaron

Aaron and I

John and I

Chapter Fourteen

DETOX AND REBIRTH

It took me many years to recover from the grief of John's death. I do not know how I did this. I knew that John would not want me to be unhappy or feel guilt. I treasured the fact that we had loved each other and spent time together. Slowly I resumed my life.

In the years after my release from prison, it had been a constant battle to get my body to function. I needed help to get through the day. Before the FDA regulations became stronger, vitamin stores sold pills that contained ephedrine, a stimulant. This pill had a lot of other ingredients, but it was better than nothing. I was a frequent patron.

Then, a few years later when I needed a physical, I went to Aris's doctor and became his patient. When he told me he would give me prescriptions for Ambien, Xanax, and phentermine, I was happily surprised. Since I was no longer using meth, I told myself I was not an addict. I started "chipping," taking just a bite, a chip off the speedy phentermine pills during the day, then Xanax and Ambien at bedtime, never knowing exactly how many pills I was taking. If I needed an extra pill to sleep, I thought nothing of it and took one. It felt good to combine the Xanax and Ambien.

When I wanted to take a nap during the day, I took a Xanax. Xanax was supposed to be a "happy" pill. It reduced anxiety, relaxed the body, and lifted a person's mood. I thought, okay, that makes me happy. But I could not control the dosage of any pill I was taking. When I took too much phentermine, my chest hurt, telling me my blood pressure was dangerously high. So I took a Xanax to bring my blood pressure and heart rate down.

When I started taking three or four Ambien a night, I knew I had a problem. Plus I was "sleep-eating" on the Ambien, getting up in the middle of the night and eating without realizing it. I would be amazed at the wrappings in the trash the next day, discovering what I had eaten because I had no memory of it. I started to gain weight, so I took more phentermine. A vicious cycle.

Cigarette smoking, diet pills, meth addiction, pills from E.J., and now a supply from a doctor; I had been an addict most of my life.

Coming out of my mourning for John, I finally realized this. I took a good hard look at myself. I was choosing to live, and I did not want to live like this.

I also knew drug addicts overdosed when they grew older because the medicine works differently on an older person. I was ready to detox. I would come clean off everything: Xanax, Ambien, and that bite of phentermine I took all day long.

Who knew Xanax and Ambien were such potent pills? I sure didn't give them any credit. Because I had quit smoking after thirty-five years and was a crystal meth survivor, I thought I could do anything.

I did not know that you should never go off any of the three drugs mentioned above, or any pills or prescriptions for that matter, without the guidance of a doctor.

Getting on my knees, I prayed, "Please, dear God. Help me overcome these terrible addictions."

I cleared my calendar of obligations for what I thought would be the next few months and went to bed.

I slept and slept, a deep unimaginable sleep.

Bam! I woke up to a body of jelly that felt like it had no bones. It was if I had been run over by a Mack truck.

At first I had a four-hour day, literally awake only four groggy hours out of each twenty-four. When I woke up, I made sure what day it was. Then I picked up my phone messages. Again, Alex, my handyman, was there to do repairs, making tenants happy, and go to the grocery store for me.

The pain and pressure on my back hurt so badly, as if I were going to burst open. It felt like someone was behind me, their very large hands on my upper arms, squeezing them, trying to hold me together.

Alex got me an old black cane. I wobbled from my bed to my couch, where I sat and looked out the window. I couldn't trust my body to do anything, and grew insecure, uncertain about what I could do. I couldn't trust my body, which was a frightening thought. I finally realized that I had approximately one hour of productive time a day.

I used the cane to get to my desk. Then I wrote checks for bills due and did paperwork, putting the envelopes at the front door for Alex to pick up.

When I went into the living room, I noticed an Amazon package on the floor. I wondered what I'd ordered, left it, and went to bed. The pile of packages grew larger. Since I wasn't able to concentrate, I grew very confused. Sometimes I thought I had sent an email. When I checked later to make sure it was sent, I might find I had sent it many times.

∷

A few months went by. On my sixty-fifth birthday, in 2012, all I had to do was get up and get ready by noon to greet my friend Suzette, who was coming to see me. I couldn't do it.

That morning, still feeling totally drugged, I dragged myself to the living room, sat on my couch, and looked at the kitchen. I thought hard about getting there.

Once I made it to the kitchen, I ate and drank something. Standing up, I made it back to the couch, then back to bed.

I finally dragged myself to the shower. I was still not ready by noon. Suzette arrived and when I opened the door, she took one look at me and said, "Call the doctor."

"No," I said. "I'm going back to sleep, I am thirsty for life now, and sleep is the only thing that matters." Slowly, slowly, I got stronger.

Gradually, my days became longer. Four hours, six hours, then eight hours. These hours would be staggered with heavy sleeping in between.

I started walking halfway down the block and back, then to the end of the block and back. Then two blocks and back, finally going around the block. Months passed, and the walks grew longer.

The air became different, smelled different. At first it smelled new and crisp, like when I was a child in Pennsylvania. Then, a few months later, the smell changed, reminding me of when I was in my twenties, in Florida. My sense of smell gradually changed to become what it is now. Without the drugs, my five senses became very acute.

Emotionally I felt as if I were different ages, at first very young, seeing my world through a child's eyes. Everything was new. I was silly, so silly, because life was fun again! This continued for almost a year. Then I was ten, then twenty, until six months later, I acted like an adult. I still have the happiness and joy of a child. I hope I never lose it.

Now my energy comes from food, not pills. This is the first time in my life that I can remember being able to focus clearly. There is day, there is night, and my body feels the rhythm. I get sleepy and go to sleep. And I love when I wake up. The first thing I say is, "Thank you, God, for healing my body, thank you for my health."

I feel so good. Nothing, no drug, nothing is better than this feeling. At last, I am the human being I was meant to be.

I am free.

A SELF-HELP GUIDE

Recently, an unhoused woman with substance abuse problems asked me how I went from being on drugs and living close to the streets to where I am now. I hope my reply can help others in a similar situation.

> Trust in God that you will be happy again.
> Go to church or place of worship of your choice.
> Talk to someone who will listen.
> Recognize that a lot of your pain comes from what you have been through and can cause you to lash back at the world in anger.
> No inner anger. Tell yourself you will channel your anger into becoming a better person. Then you will be on your way to someplace better than you are now.
> No self-destruction. Define your pain, your situation. Talk to someone and get help putting a name on your inner hurt. It is the first step to getting better.
> Try to see solutions as you are talking.
> One step at a time.
> Do one positive action a day—then two..

Love yourself.

Help other people.

Use your coping skills—what are you good at?

Make some mistakes, do better next time—keep going.

See better—know better—do better.

Don't get stuck in your story.

Forgive yourself so you can move on.

Accept the help that is offered—say thank you.

Believe in yourself. Be proud of who you are and what you were born with.

Sometimes admitting that you have an addiction is the hardest thing to do. Support can come from many sources when you open yourself up to getting help.

Everyone's journey is different. Please make some choices, small ones at first, to start you on your way. Life is choices.

YOU CAN DO IT!

THOUGHTS AFTER JOHN'S DEATH

I was given thoughts while waking up to the world. They began after John's death and continued for many months. In the morning when I woke up, I felt the thoughts in my mind. Then I got up and wrote them down.

> We each have our own spiritual path, our journey to God. We will find our own way.
> God gives us something good, a present to be thankful for every day.
> He does not give us everything all at once in our lives. It would be impossible to appreciate all things at once.
> At birth, we are given the exact amount of time we will need for the rest of our lives.
> Another person's time is valuable. Treasure it when they give it to you.
> God has a plan for you every day. It is part of your life's path.
> Everything is as it is supposed to be.
> Take responsibility for the words you speak.
> Listen to each word you are speaking as if it were you to whom you were speaking.

Live on the level of the person you are speaking with. Realize how they are looking at the world.

Be happy you are you.

God knows what is best for you. He will give you that. Sometimes it will be what you think you want, but more often, it will not. Have the wisdom to accept God's decision.

Take care of the details in your life. God will take care of the big stuff.

When pain and sorrow come, roll with the emotion. You will eventually roll yourself out of it.

All paths lead to God.

God doesn't owe me, I owe God.

Be silly like a child.

Be in the now. Watch how a dog does it.

No matter how much we figure out, work out, learn in our search for God, we are spiritual beings, living a human experience. We must live and conquer the human terrain also.

We are renting the land from Mother Earth.

When you feel grief or sadness or negative feelings come up, it is good to say, "Yes, I am feeling that," and know what you are feeling. Interestingly, we can only have one thought in our mind. It is impossible to have two thoughts at the same time. When you are ready, say, "I am going to change my thought now," and then think of something else, a thought that makes you feel better. Try this when you are depressed.

There is one God, one Spirit, and we and everything are connected to that God. It flows through us and connects us to all other beings.

Pain, joy, and suffering—you are all welcome here.

As you grow spiritually, you come to terms with money.

The constant pursuit of happiness can prevent us from enjoying the now.

People who don't want to look at the dark side are coming from fear.

Money ties us to responsibilities and we falsely think that these responsibilities will bring us happiness.

A little bit of ego is good. Just don't let it run the show.

False forces, money, politics, a profession, or fame cannot give you power.

Your family can give you power through love. Other than that, power must come from God, deep within you.

People are afraid, selfish, because they think their world might be taken away from them (death). They do not know they are the Source, and they can rebuild it.

If you're on your deathbed and your life is a mess, you made some wrong choices.

God speaks to us through other people, but usually not when they are giving us advice.

We cannot judge another person's karmic journey, nor their lifestyle or their possessions.

They are here for their own experience.

When your life isn't working, go to a shrink. Change it. Get help. Ask God for help.

All that separates us, one from another, is our thoughts. And our thoughts are just ego.

We make our own problems with poor decision-making.
    The problem will always come back to be solved.
Don't take life for granted.
We always get more than we give.
Life is precious because it is our reality now.
If you gave people all the money they wanted to buy all the things they wanted—what would they then want?
The voice of "me" is God.
An object is a thing. It's not a person, feeling, or emotion. One can take pleasure in things, but things do not bring us happiness.
You can't step into another person's karma and try to change their life. But you can make it softer.
Einstein had almost all knowledge.
Two people, thinking they have no blood connection, become grandparents and a connection is made. This is how the whole world is made—why can't we know that?
My body is what I have to carry me around in.
Ask God for help. That is prayer.
There is no such thing as a person being better or worse or above or below another person.
Mankind has created poverty, war, and illness, all unto himself.
My whole life I knew it was coming, seeing people's faults, and, of course, it is mirrors. I see my own faults in other people, reflected back to me.
Know you are exactly where you are supposed to be at this moment in time.
If you can know that, it will bring you great comfort.
People (grownups) are afraid of their bodies.

Being in love demands taking a close look at yourself.
The TV and the distractions that numb your mind do not make you think and do not make you happier. Quiet time is needed so you can look at yourself.
Look at your mind and figure out what you really think. Not what's been programmed into you.
It takes immense courage to be totally emotionally honest with yourself.
I do not have to justify myself by doing anything. I only have to sustain myself.
When we try to define ourselves by our world's definitions, it is a secondary definition. We are here to complete our life's journey, our purpose in life.
Most people never realize this and it creates unhappiness. Once you realize your purpose in life, then you know who you are.
Dying is a sweet release.
Life isn't all happy or sad each day. It's acceptance, and gratefulness to be here.
To find yourself you must face yourself.
Money is only a tool and should be respected, enjoyed, and used wisely.
I am not my body; therefore, my gender is not important to me.
You are what you eat. You are what you think. You are how you spend your time.
When a person truly loves another person, the love keeps on flowing. It may change in emotion, but it never stops.
Death brings everyone affected to a halt while they re-examine their own lives.

I am familiar with death. It is life that I question.

Most people never know who they are. They don't ask about or look at what they are thinking or feeling. They are taught by society to think within the parameters of that society.

I have been in many families in this lifetime. These people have been as close to me as my blood family.

Everything we do is all right with God.

It is how a person accepts change that determines their future, the fork in the road, the choice that's made. You can change anything you want. It's all attitude.

When people hurt you, people who love you, try to understand them and their love for you, understand *how* they love. This is the first step in forgiving them.

The more I know myself, the closer I am to God.

I am not on anyone's spiritual journey but my own.

Why anticipate? Is anything as we anticipate it to be, good or bad?

The rat race takes us away from reality. It does not produce peace, money, or good ideas.

Great thinkers, Einstein, Newton, knew there was something beyond what they were thinking and doing. They were always trying to discover this other realm of thinking.

When we know that we are Spirit having a human experience, life becomes so much easier, sweeter, happier.

Self-pity is a destructive emotion, destroying the person and relationships.

I know there are many dimensions existing simultaneously, but there is only one reality as we know it.

It's a big job being human.

Mental illness is our next frontier. We cannot see it, it is hard to explain, but it is just as much an illness as is the physical illness human beings can have.

We have taken the Earth, a big, wonderful thing, and treated it like it was Disneyland.

Unchecked emotions will override intelligence.

The way you look at the world creates your success.

Who is our enemy now? Mankind itself. It's the same enemy we have always had. Mankind and the religions we have made.

I cannot watch the thinker, myself, when I am emotional.

The body will perform miracles if the mind is understood.

When I dream, I give up my ego.

I want nothing; I have everything.

Maybe life is the other half of a circle, and we make many circles and many cycles before we are finished.

I awoke today with the knowledge that it won't be long before I get a new body.

Every stranger is ourself.

Life is our way of measuring time.

When a person has been betrayed, it is far easier for them to betray others.

Most people don't want to be challenged. They want a safe, good, easy life that, if they get it, leaves a residue of unhappiness and feeling unfulfilled.

People want more, or bigger, of the same.

If a person has no problems, there is no growth. Growth comes from how we solve those problems. This is how we make progress in our soul's growth.

There is no time. All time exists at once. I feel this.

Who listens to us think? God does.

What we have built around us that we think is our reality is what we put into being with our actions. It could all fall down, completely change.

Most people give up discovering and exploring because they see obstacles in life that seem very big. The desire to grow fades. This is the time one should change their thoughts to see the new possibilities in life.

When we change our thoughts, we build our new reality.

We all have angels. Angels are sent to us to guide us, to help us. We can call on these angels, call on them through prayer.

Who do we pray to? Jesus, Moses, Mohammed, and Allah or Most High God. They are all sons of God. We are all children of God. The same God is One. It depends on where we are born and how we are raised as to how we pray.

We are all great beings of love.

ACKNOWLEDGMENTS

A heartfelt thank you to the people who worked on this book with me.

My first copy editor, Jennifer Barclay. Her skill is much appreciated.

My second copy editor, Flo Selfman, who caught the final errors and taught me so much in the process. WordsalaMode.com

Kathleen Kaiser, whose guidance in showing me how to get the book published and her input along the way meant everything. She guided me and built a team for me that made all of this possible. KathleenKaiser.com

Jose Ramirez, who provided the services to get the book published, covering a myriad of details. His attention to detail and depth of skill made sure the book was the best it could be. His wife and partner, Barbara, had input that was key. And they were such a pleasure to work with. PedernalesPublishing.com

Adanna Moriarty of AbMoriarty Designs. Website Designer Extraordinaire! ABMoriarty.com

Mark Rowell Graphic Designer Los Angeles. He made the photos so much better.

Thank you to my friends Joanna and Jeff McAtee, who believed in me, consistently, from the start. Jeff's technical assistance and moral support, and especially Joanna's friendship and paranormal ability, anchored me during my writing. Joanna McAtee Metaphysical Counselor

To my brother Robert and his wife Sherry. And my brother Don, for confirming my memories, for his advice, and for traveling with me on my journey as only a brother and sister can do.

To my friends Louise Lawson, Suzette Ervin, Bobby Ellington, Ruth Williams, and Marcy Norton.

To all of my Facebook friends, some of whom made me realize I have benefitted from white privilege my entire life.

To all the people in this book, whether living or dead.

To everyone who was kind to me and to anyone I inadvertently forgot.

* * *

Proceeds from this book will go to People Assisting the Homeless (epath.org) and other charitable organizations.

www.ingramcontent.com/pod-product-compliance
Lightning Source LLC
Chambersburg PA
CBHW051428290426
44109CB00016B/1478